CHURCHES THAT ABUSE

CHURCHES
THAT
ABUSE

RONALD M. ENROTH

ZondervanPublishingHouse
Academic and Professional Books
Grand Rapids, Michigan

A Division of HarperCollinsPublishers

Churches That Abuse
Copyright © 1992 by Ronald M. Enroth

Requests for information should be addressed to:
Zondervan Publishing House
Academic and Professional Books
Grand Rapids, Michigan 49530

Library of Congress Cataloging-in-Publication Data

Enroth, Ronald M.
    Churches that abuse / Ronald Enroth.
        p.   cm.
    Includes bibliographical references and index.
    ISBN 0-310-53290-6
    1. Control (Psychology)—Religious aspects—Christianity—Case
studies. 2. Authoritarianism—Case studies. I. Title.
BV4597.53.C62E57 1992
262'.8—dc20   91-36097
                                                                                    CIP

International Trade Paper Edition ISBN 0-310-53299-X

Edited by Leonard G. Goss
Cover designed by The Aslan Group

Printed in the United States of America

92 93 94 95 96 97 / DH / 10 9 8 7 6 5 4 3 2 1

This edition is printed on acid-free paper and meets the American
National Standards Institute Z39.48 standard.

To
Ruth-Anne
wife, mother, friend

Contents

Preface

This has been a difficult book to write because it is a book that is critical of other Christians. One always runs the risk of being misunderstood and labeled "judgmental" or arrogant when you make evaluative statements regarding Christian believers and organizations outside your own immediate circle. The book is about churches and other Christian organizations that inflict psychological and spiritual abuse upon members through the use of fear, guilt, and intimidation.

However, when we refuse to pass judgment on any religious phenomenon for fear that such judgments might violate the norm of tolerance so prevalent in our culture, we abdicate our responsibility to the body of Christ to sound a warning where a warning is justified. Some boats need to be rocked, even Christian boats. The years of research that have gone into this book have validated for me the truth of a placard I display in my office: "Those who make it hardest to be a Christian in this world are the other Christians."

I can safely predict that not one of the groups discussed in these pages will agree that they deserve such mention. They will protest that they have been unfairly portrayed, that I have listened to "a few disgruntled former members" whose words should not be trusted, and who are not representative of the membership.

Let me assure the reader that the information I convey in this book is based not on my own fanciful imagination, but on the actual experiences of real people whose accounts can be independently verified and who, to the best of my knowledge, have been truthful about their encounters with churches that abuse. Despite the defensive protestations of authoritarian leaders that ex-members of their churches lie, distort the facts, and are "accusers of the brethren," there is abundant evidence that a serious problem of abuse exists in the Christian community.

Researching and writing *Churches That Abuse* was often a depressing experience because in recounting their days in abusive environments, the survivors I talked with had to re-live the pain and confusion, and, yes, the anger. Sometimes they were embarrassed to admit that they had allowed these things to happen to them. They felt the absence of under-standing people willing to help them "pick up the pieces."

It is my hope that this book will provide a context for understanding. If we have basic information about a subject, we can sometimes take preventative action. Regrettably, it is not always possible to "get through" to people already caught up in abusive churches. They do not see themselves as being manipulated, or in any danger of spiritual abuse. Hence, the frustration of parents, relatives, and friends who try to reach or "rescue" them. There are no easy solutions to this problem.

In the final analysis, the book presents a hopeful outlook. Not only can individuals leave abusive churches and achieve recovery and restoration, but there are encouraging signs that some groups are themselves recognizing the need for change and are moving away from the fringe toward the center. May their numbers increase.

Ronald Enroth
Santa Barbara, California
July 1991

Acknowledgments

It is customary for authors to say that without the help of many people their books could not have been written. That is especially true with regard to this book because so much of it is comprised of case histories. My greatest debt of gratitude, therefore, is to the dozens of individuals who have shared freely with me their personal, often painful, odysseys in abusive churches. Only a few of their stories can be told in these pages. But each one has contributed to my understanding of the topic and, hopefully, all will feel they have had a part in this project. I have tried to convey as accurately as possible what they have told me, but I alone am responsible for any errors.

My gratitude extends to the following people who each contributed in various ways to the success of this effort: Jamey Robertson, Kara Bettencourt, Rebecca Coons, Hubert Merchant, Betty Fleming, John Rodkey, and Anne Anderson.

I owe special thanks to Kevin Liu, whose assistance was invaluable, and for whom this book has unique meaning. I remain grateful to Herbert and Louise Moeller and to David and Dore Charbonneau for their years of encouragement. Warren and Barbara Landon demonstrated stability and caring when I felt alone. Thank you, friends.

I continue to be grateful to J. Whitney Shea, who many years ago introduced me to sociology and modeled for me not only scholarship, but Christian compassion and a steadfast faith.

Finally, I thank the staff at Zondervan Publishing House, especially my editor, Len Goss, and Zondervan's publisher, Stan Gundry. Thank you both for your supportive encouragement and your willingness to take on this topic.

1

INTRODUCTION
ABUSIVE CHURCHES:
A VIEW FROM WITHIN

1

INTRODUCTION
Abusive Churches:
A View From Within

Pastor Phil was in the stands watching his team participate in a church league softball game. The game was going great, but for some reason Pastor Phil asked the coach to substitute a number of men in the next inning. The coach complied but left the assistant pastor in the game. This evidently infuriated Pastor Phil. According to the (former) coach, "He called me with his bull horn to come to the spectator stands immediately. He was extremely angry and asked me why I had disobeyed him about the substitutions, pointing out that the assistant pastor was still in the game. Without any provocation on my part, Phil was attempting to intimidate me publicly before many people. I was stunned! His outrage continued for the rest of the evening as he attacked me and the team members."

The following week Pastor Phil was unable to attend the ball game, but he gave orders to play the game "backward." That meant the players had to bat left-handed if they were right-handed and vice versa. All field positions were switched so that everyone was playing in an unfamiliar location. Since the pastor couldn't be there, he sent someone with a camera to videotape the whole game to make sure his decree was obeyed. The point of all of this, he said, was to "humble" the team because they were getting too proud from winning so many games. The team members were, in fact, humiliated and embarrassed.

The coach later confronted Pastor Phil and told him that he was shocked and offended by his behavior. "I pointed out that I had always done what he had asked in regard to coaching any teams, and that his sudden outburst of rage toward me was totally uncalled for. His only response was that I did not obey him and therefore was not submissive to him." The coach learned later that most, if not all, of the team members had gone to Pastor Phil and apologized—even though they really had nothing to apologize for.

The scene was quite different a few weeks later when television evangelist Paul Crouch and his wife Jan were present to watch their son Matt play ball and to shoot a video spot for their Trinity Broadcasting Network. Pastor Phil was now "Mister Personality," greeting all of the players, cheering them on to victory, calling the play-by-play action while the video cameras rolled, giving "Jesus cheers," and focusing his attention on Jan and Paul Crouch. At the end of the game, he gathered the team members around him, and, ever mindful of the cameras, prayed and thanked Jesus, tears rolling down his face.

Pastor Phil is the unquestioned leader at Set Free Christian Fellowship in Anaheim, California. He likes to present the image of being a "cool" pastor. No jacket and tie for him. Wearing the obligatory sunglasses and earring, he leaps to the platform, his dark hair pulled back into a pony tail, and grabs the microphone. "I want to welcome you to Set Free Christian Fellowship—a place where people who love Jesus come, a place where people who don't know Jesus come, a place where people who want to find out about Jesus come. And it's the place, too, where a few troublemakers come, just to try to stir up trouble. I would point out a few of them right now, but I won't. We'll let God take care of them, amen?"

Then Pastor Phil invites his audience to "get high on Jesus." "Jesus Christ can just bless your brain to bits," he tells us. "Jesus Christ can make you fly. Jesus Christ can totally set you free—this morning."

As I glance around the large, old warehouse that is the setting for this 10 A.M. Sunday-worship service, I am reminded of the informal atmosphere that characterized the so-called Jesus People gatherings that I attended and wrote about in the late 1960s and early 1970s. In fact, I felt catapulted back into that time frame this late October morning in 1990 as I joined the largely youthful throng walking from all directions toward the big old building with the words SET FREE emblazoned on its side. Men from the church were directing auto and pedestrian traffic. A few people warmly welcomed me as I approached the entrance.

Before the service begins, the sounds of a Christian rock band announce to the visitor that this is no ordinary church. People are noisily milling everywhere, searching for the hard-to-find seats on the folding chairs cramped across the floor. Around the sides and back of the building, bleacher seating is also rapidly filling up.

The crowd of several thousand is composed primarily of young adults, with some people in their middle years, but very few over sixty. The audience is a mixture of Hispanics and whites, with a scattering of blacks. Quite a few children are there, many of them in the company of single mothers. Most of the folks at Set Free this morning are casually dressed—shorts or jeans, a few women displaying bare midriffs. What is especially noticeable is the presence of many males dressed in biker garb—black motorcycle vests and sleeveless denim jackets, some with "Jesus" inscribed on the back. Others proclaim, "Trained to Serve Jesus at Set Free." Beards on the men and heavy make-up on the women are the norm. Except for the biker crowd, the atmosphere is again reminiscent of the earlier Jesus People rallies, complete with the "one-way" finger sign popping up here and there throughout the audience.

The music is raucous and the crowd is enthusiastically responsive. They love the rock 'n rap gospel music. They cheer, whistle, and stomp when Pastor Phil says, "You don't have to wear a holy face here." No sir, this is California casual. Pastor Phil urges his audience, many of whom have backgrounds on "the street," to feel at home, and to forget about hymnals and fancy clothes. He promises us that we will not be hearing a three point sermon. And no poems. Just sit back, relax and enjoy "The Lord's Most Dangerous Band." "We're family," Pastor Phil reminds us.

Loud, upbeat music dominates the first half of the service. The Set Free Gospel Choir is introduced and Phil banters with his audience. "I'm gonna dedicate this in prayer for Mick Jagger that he get saved; he might be able to sing here at Set Free one of these days." The performers on the platform are "jumpin' for Jesus." One of the female vocalists sports a broad-brimmed hat that rivals the $1.98 special worn by Minnie Pearl of the Grand Ole' Opry. Other performers wear Jesus T-shirts.

Just before testimony time, Pastor Phil brings on the popular rap group, the Set Free Posse. He alerts the audience to "listen up" for the "heavy" doctrine contained in the lyrics. For those unfamiliar with the term "doctrine," he explains that in "regular" churches it means "teaching." Then he announces the title of the song: "Don't Be a Wimp!" "Wimp" is one of Pastor Phil's favorite words. From the response of the congregation, it is obvious that most of them know he is mocking traditional churches and their concern for doctrine. It soon becomes apparent how light-weight the lyrics are. The audience claps rhythmically in approval. Everyone is having a fun time.

Just before his morning talk, Pastor Phil introduces two young women who give dramatic testimony to Christian conversion. One claims that her recent past had included involvement with drugs and Satanic cults. She says that she had been a "breeder" Satanist and that one of her babies was a victim of child sacrifice.

Pastor Phil's talk is brief and undistinguished. He wants to preach the simple Gospel in a way that relates to some folks that conventional evangelical churches can't relate to or even overlook. He is effective as he stands before the crowd with open Bible in hand, informally commenting on several verses. At the conclusion of his talk, he gives an altar call and quite a few people file to the front for brief counseling and a prayer, followed by an announcement that they are now in the family of God.

Phil Aguilar, 43, does not fit the stereotype of the typical evangelical pastor. He is an ex-convict, a former drug addict, a "macho" man who rides a Harley Davidson motorcycle with a license plate that reads, "BIKER PAS," for biker pastor. His dark glasses and black leather are almost trademarks for a ministry that includes outreach to bikers and gangs ("Servants for Christ") as well as to miscellaneous street people and the homeless. As drugs increasingly penetrate the middle class, Set Free tries to minister to the young people from the more affluent suburbs. On Sunday mornings cars of all descriptions and dozens of motorcycles can be seen parked in the vicinity.

Set Free also operates a network of rehabilitation homes and ranches. Several hundred church members live in a dozen communal residences located in an area adjacent to the Set Free building. The ministry operates about twenty additional houses nearby, two of them owned by the Trinity Broadcasting Network (TBN). Most of Set Free's homes are leased at low rates from the City of Anaheim's Redevelopment Agency. Mayor Fred Hunter, an ardent supporter of Set Free, rents two houses he owns to Pastor Phil and his Set Free Christian Fellowship.

The Set Free rehabilitation program also includes small ranches located in Perris, California, one near Dallas, Texas, and another near Chicago, Illinois. These ranches, plus the urban residential program, involve approximately five hundred people. And it is this segment of Set Free ministries— the rehabilitation and communal dimension—that has stirred up controversy. Some critics have questioned the nature of the rehabilitative effort, the physical facilities themselves, and the lack of professional oversight. But most of the concern has revolved around the leadership style and suffusive influence of the man in black—Phil Aguilar. Here is an account of what happened to one couple.

Tina and Art first joined Set Free Christian Fellowship in April of 1987 because of drug and marital problems. They had hopes of a restored marriage and of starting a better life together. Pastor Phil Aguilar regularly appeared on the TBN network, announcing that anyone with problems, either drug, alcohol, or personal, could come to Set Free for counsel and assistance; no one would be turned away.

Tina and Art did go to Set Free and they were not turned away. However, by the time their stay at Set Free was over, they had divorced, Art had lost his faith and left the ministry,

Tina had remarried one of Set Free's inner circle of leaders who took her money and possessions for a drug binge and left her pregnant and alone with four other children. All of this occurred with Pastor Phil's knowledge, counsel, and blessing.

When Tina and Art first moved into the Set Free homes, they were living together in the same house and had no thoughts of separation or divorce. Soon, however, when they started to argue, they were separated by Pastor Phil into different households. They were not in agreement with this forced separation, but they submitted to Pastor Phil's supposed wisdom and discernment. According to Art, "instead of us getting together to try to work out our problems, we got separated."

Art was also not allowed to see his own children without having a permission slip. If he saw them at church, he could watch them from fifty feet away but was not allowed to talk with them. Feeling frustrated and powerless, Art watched his wife become increasingly influenced by Pastor Phil. As a young Christian, she could neither discern nor distinguish biblical truth from Set Free doctrine. She drifted further and further from her husband until, because she and Art "didn't get along," Pastor Phil counseled her to get a "worldly divorce," since a "spiritual divorce" was not possible without having committed adultery. Tina says about her experience at Set Free, "When you first start to get involved, you're so naïve about things, and it's really easy to fall into becoming part of Pastor Phil's 'clique,' especially when you're just coming off of drugs and having a lot of problems." Art adds, "At the time, Tina and I were new Christians who didn't know very much about the Lord, and we could have followed any kind of cult without even knowing it. There are a lot of people out there who twist the Word around, and there are a lot of false prophets."

At no time did Art and Tina ever receive counsel together, nor did Pastor Phil ever pray or share the Scriptures with them. Art asked many times to be able to sit down with his wife so they could talk out their problems. Each time Pastor Phil would say that they were not yet ready. Then he counseled the divorce that neither of them wanted. Tina thought that this was God's word. If Pastor Phil sanctioned the divorce, then it must be right.

Set Free claims that it ministers to many downtrodden individuals with alcohol, drug, or relational problems. Few have anything beyond a high school education. Few are Christians before coming to Set Free. According to former members and other sources, Pastor Phil himself has only two semesters of Bible school education and is very negative toward formal schooling. The theological "Master's degree" that Set Free's official spokesman claims Aguilar was awarded is in fact a certificate from a correspondence school in Florida, called International Seminary. Given this information, it is entirely understandable how individuals like Tina and Art can be swayed by Phil Aguilar's philosophy, doctrine, and practices. Tina says, "There were a lot of things Phil kept me from doing, and, at the time, I thought it was okay, but I just couldn't see what he was doing. I thought what he was doing was good for my life, and I didn't realize how bad it is to keep someone away from her family, or to keep grandchildren from seeing their grandparents." Tina wanted to leave Set Free several times. Each time she was told that she was weak and that her return to drugs was inevitable. Despite the internal struggle, she remained in the organization, fearing a return to drug abuse and godlessness.

At the time of her divorce, Pastor Phil came to Tina and told her that he cared for her, that he was with her, and that he backed her all the way in her decision to get a divorce. He also indicated that he wanted her to stay in Set Free forever and to make a life for herself there with her children. His counsel to her was to stay single for at least two years so that she could get closer to the Lord and be near her pastor. So Tina ended up living near Phil Aguilar and his family. He would frequently come to her room to talk with her whenever she was feeling down, and would tell her that she "made beautiful babies and things like that." Phil counseled her to tell her children that their father was "backslidden and not doing the things of the Lord."

Tina ended up getting remarried in Set Free to Peter, who, at the time, was one of Aguilar's lieutenants. She thought that everything was fine, but deep down began to feel that something was wrong. However, she didn't question too much because she thought that since Phil Aguilar was a pastor, anything he did had to be right. "I never questioned divorce and remarriage because I thought Phil knew what he was doing and everything was okay."

Peter and Tina also ended up leaving Set Free because they had planned on going to Hawaii for their honeymoon— without Phil's permission. Phil caused most of their wedding and honeymoon plans to be cancelled, and said that if they wanted to get sun or look at palm trees that they could spend time in the backyard of one of the Set Free houses. They ended up living in a single room with four children. Shortly after the wedding, Peter and Tina moved to another city, where Peter returned to drug abuse. In the eleven months that they were married, Peter went on four drug binges each of several days' length. The last time, he took Tina's personal possessions and money. When he returned from the last binge, he declared that he was going back to Set Free to serve God. He left on a Wednesday and on Friday he was at TBN doing phone counseling, something that Set Free members regularly volunteer to do. After that, Tina started to question God, but only, she says, "because I had made Phil my god. I couldn't understand how a pastor could allow these things to happen. I couldn't understand how Phil could allow my husband to be lifted up again right after he had just ripped off his wife and had been shooting up drugs for two days. I was pregnant at the time, and I had to have all my utilities turned off because he had stolen all my money and I wasn't able to pay our bills." The child was not planned; Pastor Phil would not allow Tina to use birth control.

Peter was received with open arms upon his return to Set Free. He was never counseled to take responsibility for his pregnant wife and children. He did attempt to return to his family but was ridiculed and mocked for such sentiments. Phil said, "Peter, you wimped out on me again." Tina and the children are still alone.

Tina's brother and mother became involved in Set Free during the same period of time that tina and Art were involved. All have been devastated. Louise, Tina's mother, joined because of her concern for her children and grand-children. A daughter-in-law and grandchildren are now lost to her. Robert, Tina's brother, went to Set Free for help with drug abuse. At this writing, Robert's wife and children are still very much a part of Set Free. He is allowed to see them for only one hour on Sundays—but only at Phil Aguilar's Set Free Christian Fellowship.

A former Set Free staff member, who came to the organization from the outside and who was filled with idealism over the possibilities for service, soon discovered nothing but frustration.

"The whole emphasis at Set Free is the idea that everybody should live in one community. However, at that particular point, my wife and I had just sold our house and had begun living in an apartment. Phil was constantly pressuring us to break our lease on the apartment and move into the Set Free homes. At that time they had twelve homes that housed about two hundred people. He said if I would move in, I wouldn't have the responsibility of having to raise any more support or have to work a part-time job in order to pay my bills, and I could be there twenty-four hours a day ministering and having the freedom to do what God called me to do. He also pointed out that if I ever had to leave town for any reason, my wife would have people to fellowship with. We became convinced that it was the right thing to do. My wife and I took that as being wisdom from the Lord and from our pastor, so we broke our lease and moved into the homes. We also sold most of our possessions. And, thinking that we would be there for the rest of our lives, we took our remaining possessions and remod-eled the home which we moved into. We gave them all of our furniture, our refrigerator, and a variety of household goods."

This was the beginning of Pat's and Kerry's ordeal as youth pastors at Phil Aguilar's Set Free Christian Fellowship. During their stay they feel they were "used" to lend an air of respectability to the Set Free ministry, were torn apart as a family, were systematically removed from responsibilities when they were becoming too successful in the youth ministry, and suffered the loss of Kerry's sister, Stacee, to the intense thought reform of the group and to Aguilar's son, Geronimo.

Pat was a youth pastor at an Anaheim church when he met Phil Aguilar. He was full of zeal for God, was considering full-time ministry, and had numerous non-traditional ideas that he believed were needed in order to reach the youth of today. He was having a hard time finding a church that would be willing to implement activities that would make church exciting and a place where young people could go and feel like they could belong twenty-four hours a day.

Pat's father-in-law introduced him to Phil Aguilar. All that they knew of Set Free at the time was that it was an inner-city ministry that helped the poor and needy and reached out to the afflicted and those in prison. According to Pat, "From the outside, everything seemed to be exactly what I was looking for." At their first meeting, Pastor Phil impressed Pat as being a very charismatic type of person. "He was very lively and full of enthusiasm. He was very non-traditional: an ex-gang member, ex-drug addict, ex-con, a Harley David-son biker who wore all black, always wore his dark Ray-Ban sunglasses without taking them off, had tattoos all over his body, and was of Mexican descent." Pat shared with Pastor Phil his vision concerning youth and his desire to open a youth center in Anaheim. He also shared with him the fact that he had a possible invitation from a church in Northern California to go and minister there. Aguilar declared that Pat would not be going there, but that God was going to call him to stay in Anaheim, and that he would ultimately be working with Set Free.

Initially discounting Pastor Phil's predictions, Pat and Kerry began attending Set Free, and, at first, it appeared to be a "real Christian utopia." Phil would call Pat's family on stage and introduce them as the "Boone family" or "the clean-cut family." This was in a congregation consisting primarily of ex-gang members, ex-drug addicts, and ex-alcoholics. Pat's family was given exceptional treatment during that initial period, and, over the course of weeks, began to grow very attached to Phil Aguilar and Set Free. Then Phil offered to make Pat Set Free's very first youth pastor. However, he would have to live by faith and raise his own support.

Immediately after this offer, Pat and Kerry were "coincidentally" visited by a member of Set Free with a word from the Lord concerning their staying in Anaheim, as well as offers of financial support. They were convinced they should stay at Set Free.

For the first three months, life and ministry were great. Pat was having great success, ministering to two hundred high schoolers and being asked to consult with state agencies. According to Pat, "Things were perfect, and we thought we had found the place that the Lord had told us to go and spend the rest of our lives." However, things changed once they decided to move into the Set Free homes.

Although Pat was eventually appointed overseer of the three main Set Free homes that housed about eighty persons, he and Kerry began to notice inconsistencies in both the Set Free Fellowship and in Phil Aguilar's life. The red lights began to go on. Phil surrounded himself with non-educated and court-appointed individuals needing supervision. Many could not read and depended on Phil for teaching and the interpretation of Scripture. These persons were not afforded any education at Set Free and, according to Pat, they "literally fear Phil and they serve Phil." New Christians would be sent to TBN (the Trinity Broadcasting Network) to staff the telephone counseling lines—a "blessing" that was required of Set Free members, even if they were not yet completely free of their own addictions. Any questioning of Phil's decisions or any indications of "irresponsibility" resulted in a stay at "the Ranch," a five-acre dirt facility outside of Perris, California, consisting of a few ten-by-ten-foot modular rooms and an outdoor wood-heated shower.

The times away from Set Free at the ranch were ordinarily set aside for spiritual growth, a place where "you could go to be closer to the Lord." But sometimes it was used just as a place of punishment. Phil would separate parents and children by sending young children, he would separate husbands and wives by sending one or the other, and he would separate mothers, daughters, brothers, and sisters. People put up with such treatment and stayed with Set Free because many knew that if they left, they would not have anywhere else to go.

Things were no more consistent with the Scriptures in Aguilar's personal life, Pat soon learned. While claiming that he had taken a vow of poverty and that he had had to move forty-two times in his ministry, he would go out to eat lunch and dinner frequently, wear fifty dollar shirts, outfit his children in expensive shoes and clothing, and buy various accessories for his motorcycles. Meanwhile, Pat and Kerry's weekly food budget for the twenty-five persons in their communal house was two hundred dollars. Phil also had access to many different motorcycles and cars. He headed up car and motorcycle "ministries" and would give motorcycles to devoted followers so that they could participate in these church-sponsored "outreach" activities. To downplay his expensive habits, Aguilar would dress in cutup t-shirts, shorts, and army boots, according to Pat.

Perhaps reflecting on his own meager theological education, and revealing his personal feelings of inadequacy, Pastor Phil would sometimes comment that "the only thing worse than an old Christian was an educated Christian." Yet, he would discipline his followers by calling them "spineless wimps," "babies," or "uneducated." He would sometimes ridicule and humiliate people in public.

Personal quirks also resulted in inconsistency in practices as well as doctrine. Persons seeking assistance at Set Free received differential treatment according to their connections with influential people and how much they could benefit Pastor Phil. Pat's youth ministry was severely curtailed when the former youth director, an influential and financially supportive woman, wanted her position back. Pat and Kerry believed that their family was being used as a public relations tool to further Pastor Phil's ministry and offset his biker image.

Pat and Kerry's relationship with Kerry's parents was severely strained to the point that, at the end of their time with Set Free, they were told essentially that Kerry would have to choose between her parents or the Set Free ministry. Kerry's parents could only see their grandchildren when they worked as nursery volunteers on Sunday. They were labeled as being a hindrance to the work of God.

Kerry's sister, Stacee, is still a member of Set Free, having married Phil Aguilar's son, Geronimo. She has been turned against her family, and, on several occasions when visiting with Stacee, Kerry and Pat have been told that they "stir up trouble" and "cause division" by wanting to see her. They feel that Stacee has succumbed to the "Christian macho" environment promoted by the Aguilars. She is "supposed to treat her husband as if he were the Lord," according to Pat. She was up, serving her husband food and drink, hours after the birth of their first child. Her husband does not participate in the care of the baby, preferring to wait until the time the child can communicate with him. Speaking of her brother-in-law, Kerry observes: "He continually goes off and does whatever he wants, which usually doesn't include Stacee." Stacee continues to defend and build up her husband. A common complaint of former Set Free members is that many of the men in the church treat women like doormats.

Phil allows no elders in the church, claiming that he alone is responsible before God for all of his flock. Thus, internal accountability is nullified. Also, as shepherd of the communal flock, Phil requires permission notes for all aspects of life. Pat was not allowed to oversee his family as husband and father, but was expected to consult with Phil on all matters.

According to Pat, because of these and other areas of disagreement, "I finally got to the point where I was about to lose my wife and child. Kerry was being tormented psychologically and was increasingly negatively affected by the ministry." Eventually, Pat was taken to a football practice to be told that he was being a "wimp" because he wasn't able to control his wife and keep her away from her mother. He was told that he had to decide whether he was going to be in control of his family and "get some guts," or leave the ministry. After consulting with two other Set Free leaders who also admitted that they had considered leaving, Pat was told that if he was going to leave he must do so very quietly so that he didn't stir up any problems.

One evening Pat and his wife did leave very quietly, but

when they returned to pick up their furniture, they found that everything had been removed from their room and locked up. As they began to load what was left of their belongings, Pastor Phil came by to help them pack. Here is Pat's account of what followed.

"I told him that he didn't have to help us. His response was that the sooner he got us out of there the better. After we had loaded everything, he began to verbally attack me, hoping to get me to physically attack him. He began to discredit me by calling me a spineless wimp and a baby. He said that I was sowing discord in the ministry and causing other people to leave. When I responded using Scripture, he didn't answer, but continued to belittle me in front of my wife and all the people in the homes. I am sure he was trying to provoke me to anger so that I would physically attack him. That would prove to all the observers that I was indeed an 'outlaw,' which is Set Free jargon for a backslider or a rebellious person."

Six months after Pat and Kerry left to become involved in another Christian ministry elsewhere in the state of California, they returned to Set Free to visit Kerry's sister, Stacee, who was now pregnant with her first child. Phil eventually showed up and the first thing he said to Pat was, "Hello, el wimpo. Wimpo is back in town." He came up to Pat, gave him a hug, and asked him what he was doing there. "I told him that I was just visiting and then he told me that I better leave right away. He again said that I was trying to sow discord. He called me a loser and a spineless wimp. He proceeded to inform me how God wasn't doing anything with my life and how miserable I was. He said that my family life was down the tubes and that was the reason I was back in town. After a few more minutes of his verbal abuse, Phil's secretary, Lois, joined in and began to tell me that I was treading on dangerous ground. She said that if I continued to act that way toward Phil, God would probably take my life because I was messing with a man who was anointed by God."

As Pat tells it, Phil became even angrier. "He started to pat me on the head and make some kissing gestures at me. Then he came up and kissed me right on the lips and said, 'Now what are you going to do about that?'" Pat told Phil that he would pray for him because he was really confused and that God was going to deal with him severely if he chose to continue on his present path. That was the last time Pat and Kerry saw Pastor Phil Aguilar.

It is Pat's opinion that "Phil Aguilar is a very confused individual who is selfish, chauvinistic, prideful, jealous, arrogant, and extremely authoritarian. He will do anything to advance his organization, his ministry, or his business." Before Phil became a Christian, he was nicknamed "King Cobra." The day that he kissed Pat on the lips, Pat remarked that the "Cobra" had never died, but still lived on. Pastor Phil turned, looked at Pat, and walked away.

———————————•◆•———————————

This book is about people who have been abused psychologically and spiritually in churches and other Christian organizations. Unlike physical abuse that often results in bruised bodies, spiritual and pastoral abuse leaves scars on the psyche and soul. It is inflicted by persons who are accorded respect and honor in our society by virtue of their role as religious leaders and models of spiritual authority. They base that authority on the Bible, the Word of God, and see themselves as shepherds with a sacred trust. But when they violate that trust, when they abuse their authority, and when they misuse ecclesiastical power to control and manipulate the flock, the results can be catastrophic. The perversion of power that we see in abusive churches disrupts and divides families, fosters an unhealthy dependence of members on the leadership, and creates, ultimately, spiritual confusion in the lives of victims.

And victims they are. In this book you will meet some of the casualties of spiritual abuse. They will tell you in their own words why they were attracted to authoritarian religious groups and what the impact of that involvement has meant. They will share the pain of leaving an abusive church and the struggle to readjust to life on the "outside." For many of them, life in an all-encompassing Christian environment has been so devastating that they find it difficult sometimes to read their Bibles, attend church, or even believe in God.

Much has been written about battered wives and child abuse. Here you will read about battered believers and abused Christians. The people in this book, for the most part, define themselves as born-again Christians. The churches and leaders that abused them are evangelical or fundamentalist in theological orientation. However, churches that abuse are on the margins, or just outside the circle, of the mainstream evangelical subculture as it exists in North America. That is, they would not ordinarily seek membership in organizations like the National Association of Evangelicals or financially support missionary and humanitarian organizations such as World Vision International. Their children would not participate in Young Life or Youth for Christ, and they would not encourage their young people to attend mainstream evangelical colleges like Westmont and Wheaton, or even Bible schools like the Moody Bible Institute. Their pastors would not read *Christianity Today* magazine.

I have spent several years researching this book and have interviewed hundreds of abuse victims in order to learn about their experiences. I have also talked with many other people whose lives have touched former and current members. I have used a tape recorder consistently, but not always. As much as possible in this book, I want to convey the feelings, the attitudes, and the experiences of the people themselves—in their own words—a view from the inside. There will be a minimum of analysis and commentary. In terms of methodology, my mentor is Harvard social psychiatrist Robert Coles, author of the celebrated series *Children of Crisis*. Like him, my aim is "to approach certain lives, not to pin them down, not to confine them with labels, not to limit them with heavily intellectualized speculations but. . .to approach, to describe, to transmit as directly and sensibly as possible what has been seen, heard, grasped, felt. . . ."[1]

Each chapter contains one or more case studies as well as anecdotal material from interviews and other sources. Occasionally I have presented a composite case history; that is, I have combined two or three people into one individual. Sociologists are concerned about the validity and reliability of their data. I feel that the case studies presented here are reasonably representative. I believe that the people who shared their experiences with me were being truthful and I am equally certain that the leaders of their former churches would assert that these ex-member accounts are exaggerated or, at the least, distorted. Although I did not use formal questionnaires and do not claim that my findings have any "statistical significance," I feel that I have identified patterns of behavior that can be independently verified using standard behavioral-science methodology.

In addition to employing informal, in-depth interviews of former members, I have visited some of the churches mentioned, listened to countless hours of taped sermons and talks by the pastors under discussion, and talked with relatives and friends of individuals who are currently members of such groups. Whenever possible, I have attempted to interview those in leadership. In all but a few instances, I identify the pastors and churches referred to in this book by their actual names. The names of all former members have been changed.

Sociologists look for patterns in human behavior and in social institutions. As you read the following pages, a profile of pastoral and spiritual abuse will emerge. Abusive churches, past and present, are first and foremost characterized by strong, control-oriented leadership. These leaders use guilt, fear, and intimidation to manipulate members and keep them in line. Followers are led to think that there is no other church quite like theirs and that God has singled them out for special purposes. Other, more traditional evangelical churches are put down. Subjective experience is emphasized and dissent is discouraged. Many areas of members' lives are subject to scrutiny. Rules and legalism abound. People who don't follow the rules or who threaten exposure are often dealt with harshly. Excommunication is common. For those who leave, the road back to normalcy is difficult.

The patterns of abuse, the mechanisms of response and coping, and the similarities in outcome have become clear to me as I have attempted to understand the phenomenon of authoritarian churches. At times, when hearing a person's odyssey for the first time, I am tempted to say, "Stop, let *me* tell *you* the rest of the story." I am reminded of a comment made by Robert Coles regarding his research experience. He notes that "some observations and considerations keep coming up, over and over again—until. . .they seem to have the ring of truth to them. I do not know how that ring will sound to others, but its sound after a while gets to be distinct and unforgettable to me."[2]

2

FRINGE AND FANATICISM
ABUSIVE CHURCHES CAN
GO OVER THE EDGE

2

FRINGE AND FANATICISM
Abusive Churches
Can Go Over The Edge

On March 20, 1986 Janet Cole drove from Seattle to Portland and drowned her five-year-old daughter, Brittany, in a motel bathtub. The attractive thirty-seven-year-old mother, described by friends as the ideal Christian woman, was convinced that she was demon possessed and that a similar fate would probably befall her daughter. She wanted the little girl to go to heaven and so committed an act of love by killing her.

Janet Cole was also a member of a large Pentecostal church, Community Chapel, in south Seattle that ex-members and other critics claim was pre-occupied with demons and "deliverance ministry." The tragic drowning resulted in the first of a series of media reports that brought unwanted publicity to the church and its former pastor, Donald Lee Barnett. In addition to the emphasis on exorcism, a swirl of controversy emerged as a result of Barnett's teaching on "intimate dancing" and "spiritual connections" with members of the opposite sex.

Barnett claims that this "move of God" had its origin in a series of mystical experiences he had, including an encounter with a "dancing angel." His "revelation teaching" was derived in part from a heavenly vision in which God told him that he would give him truth that he had not given to any man before. "God let me know that no man had entered that highest realm that I saw. He allowed me to experience things that no man has ever seen. I was connected with God; I had revelation, I was one with Jesus Christ."

Robin and Matt were two people who were swept away by Pastor Barnett's "revelational teaching." Their lives have never been quite the same since. They are among dozens of people I have interviewed at length about the almost unbelievable events that transformed Community Chapel from an unknown church on the fringe of fundamentalism into a fanatical, spiritually abusive organization. You will find it difficult to believe that what happened to Robin and Matt is quite typical of the upheaval experienced by hundreds of other people in this "move of God."

"I'd call Jen [a friend in the church], screaming, crying, because I knew what I was experiencing was spiritual; I knew there was deception somewhere. But I didn't know where or how I was being deceived. The church was pulling me one way, Matt was pulling me one way, my own heart was saying something else, my husband was in love with one of my best friends and she was now living upstairs with him. I had had some surgery, and I was distraught. So I ended up living in the basement going out of my mind, while they played mom and dad upstairs and took care of the kids. I was like Cinderella in the cellar, losing my bananas. Matt would, sometimes in the middle of the day, come home and come to my house to take care of me. He ended up staying with me every night because I couldn't sleep. I was skin and bones. I couldn't eat; I couldn't sleep; my skin got bad; my hair started falling out. I was tormented, and I was planning and plotting how I could murder my children and take my own life to get out of the insanity, because I was in love and totally dependent for my sanity upon a married man who had two children."

This was the culmination of Robin and Matt's story of their many years of involvement with Donald Lee Barnett's Community Chapel. Barnett, 62, began Community Chapel in 1966 as a small, basement Bible study. By the mid 1980s, attendance at Sunday services was over two thousand, not including the network of twelve satellite churches that were at one time associated with Community Chapel. Today, the Chapel is only a shadow of what it was in the 1970s and

1980s. Membership has dwindled to about two hundred, legal battles have divided the congregation, the pastor is gone, and part of the church property has been sold to pay bills. What is described here is the Chapel at its zenith, just before its collapse. It's the incredible story of what can happen when a church becomes abusive and slides toward spiritual and moral chaos, when a church already on the margins of conventional evangelicalism goes beyond the fringe.

The organization had a ten-million-dollar complex where members, including Robin and Matt, not only learned about God and the Bible, but spent hours in protracted "intimate dancing" with their "spiritual connections." As a result of this church and its pastor, Robin and Matt are now divorced from their spouses, separated from their children, and married to one another.

Members of Community Chapel were instructed by Barnett about every aspect of life, spiritual and temporal. Church bulletins frequently included "pastoral admonitions" that were unusual. For example, one Sunday bulletin warned men against using unisex styling salons. "Our church stands opposed to any hair style on men which tends toward the mod, rebellious, or effeminate! As pastor I am very much against a fad that is growing for men to get permanents at unisex styling salons. Please do not identify with the effeminate, unisex, homosexual fashion trends. Mothers: even though it may be convenient, it is unwise to take young boys to the beauty shop (or unisex styling salon) for their haircuts. While there, they will see the 'big boys' getting their fancy, poofy, effeminate hairstyling. Years of such practice could cause them to be ensnared, too. These places are not without homosexual demons just waiting to influence the gullible." Seminars offered by the church leadership covered topics like, "How to Keep Your Yard," "Masturbation," "Child Rearing," "Dress Standards," "How to Be a Good Wife," "How to Be a Good Employee," "How to Be a Minister's Wife," "How to Choose Make-up."

If there is just one word to describe Don Barnett and his church, it would be "control"—autocratic control over the lives of the individual members. Barnett's pastoral "concerns" went so far as to dictate how close together people should sit in the pews of the church. He also expressed concern in a church bulletin over the fact that he had received "reports of a number of people experiencing insomnia night after night for no apparent reason." Among other things, he recommended that his parishioners take a hot bath immediately before bedtime, along with some warm milk. "Ask the Lord, in faith, for a good night's sleep; taking authority over physical, emotional, and possible demonic influences. Then let your body go limp." The advice was signed, "Your pastor who cares for you."

That "care" also extended to divorced persons and the question of dating. "Because the potential for sin, abuse, and demonic attack in this area is immense, we must maintain a strong position in order to uphold godliness, and insure as far as is reasonable none among us is overly hurt." Therefore, members of Community Chapel were asked to comply with the following two rules "in order to be in this church": "(1) A divorced person may not date or begin building a relationship with a member of the opposite sex without first obtaining permission to date from the pastor. Address your request for such permission to his wife, to whom he has delegated oversight in this area; (2) Nobody who is in the process of separating or divorcing may date or begin to build a new relationship with a person of the opposite sex. No exceptions."

Most members experienced a totalitarian system of control in which all free time, outside of employment, was given to the "assembly," or church. The epitome of being spiritual, in fact, was to have a job at Community Chapel. Most evenings were given to church activities. It was not at all unusual to spend five or six nights a week in church. When asked what members did for fun, Robin responded, "That is what we did for fun, we went to church."

Community Chapel had not always been so controversial and controlling, although its pastor had promoted various unorthodox concepts from the beginning. As a youngster, Barnett and his family belonged to the United Pentecostal Church, a small denomination isolated from the Christian mainstream because of its rejection of the traditional concept

of the Trinity. Barnett still preaches a non-trinitarian message.

Although never ordained a minister, he did attend an
unaccredited Bible seminary in Idaho and began his ministry as a Sunday school and Bible study teacher in a series of
Assemblies of God churches in Washington. Barnett left each
of these churches because of doctrinal disagreements. Meanwhile, he worked as a draftsman.

By 1967, Barnett and his wife Barbara began a home Bible
study that attracted newly born-again Christians eager for
fellowship. The group quickly grew; the Friday-night "Sing-
spirations" and Barnett's approach and teachings were
attractive to new converts. As one former member says, "The
teaching didn't seem bad at first. He was preaching the
Gospel and the church was growing. But everyone who came
in was a new Christian and they didn't know the Word of
God. Everything they knew came through Barnett's teaching, and they had to totally submit to him."

The Friday-night Bible study grew into a church with a
Bible school, funded largely by the sacrificial offerings of its
members. Early services at the chapel were fairly typical of
Pentecostal services, including speaking in tongues, and
"words of knowledge" from God. As the church grew and the
number of employees increased, Barnett's sense of power
and need for control grew accordingly, say former members.

Barnett instituted "Operation Rescue" in which members
were instructed to report each other's faults to the pastor. A
dress code for both men and women was also begun, as well
as a dietary code restricting pork, shellfish, and alcohol, all
based on Barnett's interpretation of the Old Testament laws.
Oreo cookies were outlawed because they contained lard.
Interracial dating was proscribed. Certain Christian books
and bookstores were to be avoided because they promoted
"false" creeds. However, Barnett approved of and quoted
from a weekly publication by a neo-Nazi group.

Celebrating Christmas and Easter was discouraged because Barnett considered them secular holidays. Engage-
ments could not be announced until Barbara, the pastor's
wife, was informed. Every indication of a negative or

"rebellious" attitude or unapproved opinion was attributed to demons.

By the time Robin and Matt became involved in 1972, Barnett was beginning to promote the first in a series of "corporate moves of God." The first was the "white room experience," introduced by Barbara Barnett as a result of a vision she supposedly received from God. This mystical place enabled one to become especially intimate with the Lord, but could only be reached through a progression of different stages of spiritual maturity. Robin recalls that there was much talk about it and other "super-spiritual" experiences by people who had access into the white room.

This was only one of many spiritual fads that would sweep through the Chapel, exciting many of the faithful but confusing many others. For example, there was the "pillar of holiness" movement, but, "if you didn't get into the white room, then you couldn't get into the pillar of holiness." This was followed by additional waves of highly emotional experiences, including "singing in the Spirit" in which the congregation would sing in tongues together. Then there was something called "spiritual surgery" in which individuals were encouraged to "completely yield to God," so that inner healing could result. This was accompanied by individuals being "slain in the Spirit," a phenomenon common in some Pentecostal circles in which persons so overwhelmed by God appear to faint away in a trance-like state.

Finally, "dancing before the Lord" was instituted in 1983, the precursor to "intimate dancing" and "spiritual connections." A former elder and Community Chapel Bible College teacher offers this explanation as to what happened: "We put a premium on spiritual experience. It's shocking to me to see what transpired. Once you're out in the realm of experience, you can't talk Scripture anymore because there's no Scripture that's relevant to something as wild and bizarre as this."

Robin compares these so-called movements of God to the story of *The Emperor's New Clothes*: ". . .nobody wants to confess that they're the only one in the group that doesn't have any clothes on, so they just kind of jump on the band wagon. They get into it even if it doesn't seem right to them because they don't want to miss out on what God has for them. They don't want to be left out of 'the bride,' left out of the 'rapture,' not be part of the 'man-child ministry.'" She believes that these fears of losing out are real to the people involved and that Barnett used the fear along with heavy doses of guilt and emotional manipulation to control the congregation. "Everyone was ready to go for anything that seemed spiritual."

Matt believes that these spiritual and emotional experiences over the past years were the key community builders of the church. They drew the people closer through shared experience. However, they have also left individuals terribly confused and families sometimes broken beyond repair. The practice of "spiritual connections" had a particularly demonic impact. There were numerous accounts of adulterous relationships, sexual assault, harshly shunned and rejected dissidents, child abuse, suicides and attempted suicides, broken marriages, child-custody battles, and lawsuits, several of which were aimed at Pastor Barnett for alleged sexual misconduct.

Robin reports that Chapel women had a reputation around the Seattle area as the women who walk around in a trance. Some of them worked in the food-service department of a major hotel where the other workers viewed the Chapel Christians negatively. One of the waitresses said, "We can't even stand to work with them because they're out to lunch. They've got a loose screw somewhere, and they don't pull their share of the weight. They're off in unreality somewhere."

The "moves of God" at Community Chapel did indeed leave many in just such a state of unreality. The dramatic and ever-accelerating barrage of sensual and spiritual experience caused many people to have their discernment ability dulled to the point of no longer being shocked at anything. As one former member put it, "Unless it was horrible, perverted, kinky sex or adultery, or somebody sexually abusing a kid, I was not shocked anymore by it." Exposure to extremes of behavior and belief at Community Chapel had desensitized members to the point where conscience and morals were anesthetized.

Contributing to this state of unreality among members of

Community Chapel was what psychologists call the "double bind" theory of mental dysfunction. "We were told one thing and then what is done is totally opposite, and so you're trying to redefine terms to apply to something that is not real." Robin gives the example of Barbara, Don Barnett's wife. Barbara was held up as a model for Community Chapel women. While Barnett preached that "you don't want to draw undue attention to yourself. . .you want to look feminine, and you don't want to dress in a seductive way. . .," his wife presented a different image. According to Robin, "She wore a wig, she had false eyelashes; she wore spiked heels. . .you see her on the street and people turn around and gape and stare." In the view of some Chapel parishioners, the pastor's wife looked more like the prostitute Jezebel than the godly wife of Proverbs 31.

Community Chapel women were expected to dress in very feminine attire, not the "jeans and sloppy shirts" that "worldly women" were seen in. Barnett reportedly told the congregation, "It may come to the point in this world where the only women who dress in a feminine way are the prostitutes." Matt says that because of this and many other irreconcilable contradictions, "our friends were going insane."

"Connections" and "intimate dancing" nearly caused Robin to have a mental breakdown. Instituted between 1983 and 1985, the "dancing before the Lord" evolved into a teaching with specific rules that encouraged members to find a "connection," or dance partner. Soon partners were instructed to stare into one another's eyes, eventually known as "connecting." Partners were told they would see Jesus in each other's eyes, and that they were to love their spiritual connection in order to express the love of Jesus. During the week, both in church and outside the church, members were encouraged to spend time with their spiritual connections in a kind of quasi-dating relationship. As might naturally be expected, physical intimacy often accompanied these "spiritual" connections. "Connection love" was supposedly more intense, and even more desirable, than marital love.

Robin graphically describes what it was like at church during sessions of intimate dancing. "Picture your typical forty-year-old wife who's out of shape and has six kids. There she is watching her husband dancing with this little twenty-year-old perfect beauty—long blonde hair, big bust, little waist—in his arms, gazing at her for hours. And meanwhile the wife is going insane." Spouses were taught that they had to "release their mates unto the Lord" if they experienced feelings of jealousy. At the same time, Pastor Barnett made clear from the pulpit, they were not to view the connections "carnally." What the people were doing physically—hugging, holding, fondling, kissing—was not to be viewed with the eyes of the "flesh." "What's happening is they're having spiritual union," said the pastor. "It just looks the same on the outside, but what's really occurring is spiritual, so don't judge them or their motives."

God, it was said, was using the connections to break down the barriers and inhibitions within the congregation in order to bring about greater "unity within the body." "We're gonna fall in love with everyone," was the message. Although this inevitably led to marital friction, the members were told that intimate spiritual experiences with members of the opposite sex, other than one's spouse, could help defeat the demons of jealousy and open up the person to a deepened experience of the love of Christ. Participants were actually instructed to diversify. "Don't commit yourselves to any one person." It was not unusual for members, including the pastor and his wife, to connect with more than one person at a time.

Those considered most spiritual were invited to dance in the front of the church with Barnett. All his connections were described as "beautiful, well-endowed, and young." Robin and Matt believe that Barnett "obviously has some sort of sexual problem. . . . He's so preoccupied with women's bodies." Barnett discussed oral sex in Sunday school and was "inappropriately explicit" regarding sexual matters from the pulpit.

Community Chapel has reportedly paid for abortions for members, including teenagers, and Barnett has preached that "God never did really say 'thou shalt not have an abortion.'" Those who say abortion is murder are said to be guilty of a "legalism," a term used to refer to an incorrect or overly literal interpretation of biblical, civil, or moral law. He reasoned that if "adultresses" were forced to have babies, the children raised by them, or given up for adoption, would grow up to lead sinful lives and end up in hell. If aborted, they would return to God.

Robin and Matt say that the extreme emphasis on sexual issues impacted the children and adolescents of Community Chapel in one of two ways. "Either they were really into it or they think it's junk." The entire eighth grade class at the church's Christian school refused to have dancing chapels because they believed that it was "ridiculous." Matt is afraid that an entire generation is being lost because of Community Chapel's aberrant former pastor.

———————•◆•———————

What went wrong at Community Chapel? How can one explain the bizarre series of events that led to Barnett's eventual downfall? According to former members Robin and Matt, "Don Barnett lost his grip on the Bible. It was that Book which kept the place reasonably sober over the years. He gradually diminished and de-emphasized the Bible as something to preach from, as something to live by. He had to get rid of the Book."

Much of the problem can also be attributed to the deceptive nature of Barnett's sensual theology. He and his wife, over a period of several years, drew the congregation into the trap of believing that the sexual and the spiritual realms were innocuously intertwined. Barnett increasingly relied on mystical and subjective religious experience to convince his followers that he was indeed in touch with God. He gradually, cleverly, and subtly prepared his audience for what would be considered outrageous pronouncements in more conventional evangelical churches.

One such bizarre event took place in 1983 when Barbara Barnett shared a vision she supposedly received from God. Robin was present when the pastor's wife told the story and here is her account of what transpired.

"Barbara had a vision of herself standing before the Lord, and we, her spiritual children, were all there. As she was standing before the Lord, he asked her to disrobe and come to him. She was very embarrassed and reluctant to do so, but she said, 'I never say no to Jesus. I always obey him and so I just fixed my gaze on him and knew I could do anything he asked.' She started to disrobe and then he asked her to dance and come to him. So she started to dance. He took her into a chamber and she said, 'Oh, I'm so glad to be alone with you, Lord.' And he said, 'No, I want them to come too.' She said, 'Oh, I just don't know how I can do it; it's just way too hard. But I knew that Jesus wanted me to.' He then lay her down on this beautiful bed that was strewn with rose petals. As she was lying there, she looked at the walls and ceiling and they were covered with flowers. He was beginning to make love to her when she noticed that each flower was a face—a face of a person from the congregation. She was mortified at first, but he said, 'I want you to be willing to let them watch you yield to me so that they can learn how to do it.' Barbara went on to say, 'There's nothing sexual about this at all, there's nothing romantic. It's just a picture of what is occurring spiritually when you yield your heart to the Lord.'"

Most evangelical Christians would probably conclude that Barbara Barnett had an occultic experience rather than an encounter with the Jesus of the Bible. It was this kind of mystical experience, elaborated on in countless sermons by the pastor, that set the stage for the congregation to believe that they could encounter Jesus through other individuals. Jesus was identified with the men of the assembly, and the women constituted the bride.

As the teaching about spiritual connections began to evolve, people were told that they could even experience a kind of mystical union with their connection while making love to their spouse. "It is so far beyond anything that anyone has experienced sexually that we know it's spiritual," said one of Community Chapel's elders. Other members have reportedly communicated with the spirits of their absent connections, and been made love to by their connections who "embodied" their spouses. Some have danced with the spirits of deceased members. Barbara has also testified about having connections with David, Abraham, and Moses.

Matt and Robin say they have experienced the "demonic, occultic power" of the connection phenomenon. They believe that it is more than just people "going insane, becoming schizophrenic, or making it up." The people involved in what were termed "mega" or main connections (primary pairings), supposedly experienced the greatest power. Matt says, "It's not just people having infatuations or even just falling in love. It was an intensely psycho/spiritual experience. I couldn't live without her [Robin]. I couldn't work; I couldn't eat; I was literally out of my mind."

Matt describes how it all got started. "Though I'd attended church there for eight years or so, I never knew Robin. I had jumped into this latest 'move of God' right away, something that was not unusual for me to do. Anyway, I was doing a lot of dancing with a lot of people and Robin first came and said she'd like to dance with me. That's how it happened. I danced with Robin, maybe twenty minutes, and I was so hooked on what I had experienced that, well,. . . . We were both married at the time. It's so difficult to describe the intense emotions, the passion, the longing.

"I consider it entirely or almost entirely demonic. We knew at the beginning that we were surrounded by demonic power. We sensed it, but we couldn't define it."

Robin's children suffered as a result of the connecting experience. She says, "The kids went through hell." She believes that she was literally going out of her mind at that time and would have benefited from "involuntary incarceration" if there had been some way to provide for the children. Her ex-husband and his "connection" took on the child-care responsibilities.

An interesting postscript is that in Robin's opinion, those who were considered to be the most spiritual at Community Chapel and who supposedly had the most contact with God were those who had come out of deep occult backgrounds. Those persons who resisted getting involved in the dancing phenomenon were told that their refusing to dance was the result of "demonic oppression."

As for herself, Robin said, "I was having lots of supernatural experiences; I assumed and was quite sure it was all of God." Although it took her a year to get herself to dance in the congregation, she finally began when she saw a nine-teen-year old dancing. "I felt like I was Jesus and I saw him as the bride, and I thought, 'I've gotta get to him; I've gotta dance with him.'" She danced for four straight hours and felt that when she looked at him, she was "looking right into the eyes of Jesus. . . . I felt totally free to be vulnerable to Jesus through him, and I had this powerful experience with the Lord while dancing with him." Now she is not sure if it was Jesus of Nazareth that she saw in her partner's eyes, or *his* voice that spoke through this man while she danced with him, telling her of things that no one could know. "Every time I would look at this guy, especially if I'd look at his right eyebrow. . . . I could see Jesus looking through his eye at me. We didn't have a physical relationship at all, but it was an intense emotional bonding." Robin also states that the connecting experience was so intense that she and other women would experience orgasm without ever having any physical contact with their connections.

Robin's connection with Matt was at first just an "intense spiritual union. . .there was nothing physical at all about it, not a shred, but we became locked into each other, and I've been with him every single day since. We could not stay away from each other. We became so emotionally tied, and I'm not talking just infatuated and wanting to be together, I mean not being able to live. It got to the point where he would leave for work, and then he'd call me as soon as he'd get there, and I'd be OK. He'd work for maybe ten or fifteen minutes and then he'd go in and he'd call me up again. By the time he got to me on the phone, I was an emotional wreck, crying, totally confused, out of my mind. He'd talk to me for ten, fifteen, maybe thirty minutes, and get me sane again."

Robin and Matt finally escaped Community Chapel and Don Barnett. They are now married to one another and Robin is pursuing a doctorate in counseling psychology.

What contributed to Community Chapel's slide into what observers agree is false teaching and deception? Virtually all ex-members agree with the conclusion of a founding elder of the church that an over-emphasis on experience began a drift away from the Bible. "It was the experience focus that got us off the track more than any other thing." "People need to be reminded," commented another former member, "not to put their confidence in a set of criteria put forth by a man who is simply relating his observations, but to place their confidence squarely on the Bible as the only infallible standard for judging truth."

The tragedy of Community Chapel goes back to a misplaced loyalty. People, thinking that they were placing their allegiance in the Word of God, were actually placing their allegiance in a man and his interpretation of the Word of God. That is crucial to understanding why people were so easily deceived. They *thought* that they were really obeying the Word of God.

The comments of a former elder who was associated with the church for eighteen years before resigning are insightful: "As I look back on it now, it is clear that, subtly at first, there began to be a feeling of superiority and exclusiveness among the people. This was more evident in some than in others, but I think we all were affected by it. There began to be a feeling that this church was unique, and that while we loved other brothers in Christ, to leave Community Chapel would always be a step down spiritually.

"The pastor rarely had other preachers in to minister to us, feeling that they really couldn't add anything to us, and might only foster divisions and problems. I feel that this is one of the critical factors in the sad things that happened later: no checks and balances with the rest of God's people, and no accountability to other men of God outside our own little circle."

Quite clearly, the excesses at Community Chapel demonstrate what can happen when spiritual experience dictates theology and then necessitates a re-interpretation of Scripture. Subjective experience takes care of the theological loopholes that the Bible seems not to address. The leadership of Community Chapel promoted the view that one could accept certain doctrines and practices if they could not be *disproved* from Scripture, rather than accept them because of a strong conviction they were right because they were taught in God's Word. It has been said that commitment without careful reflection is fanaticism in action, and that certainly was the case at Community Chapel.

Another problem was the abdication of personal moral responsibility for sin, blaming it instead on the work of demons. There was a tendency to attribute any problem, interpersonal or otherwise, to demons. Members would spiritually psychoanalyze one another with regard to what specific demons were troubling them and then point to the need for "deliverance." This would be the case frequently between marriage partners. Common, natural emotions were more often than not attributed to demons. Members were told that when they saw their spouses dancing in an intimate manner with some other person, they were not to feel any jealousy, resentment, or hurt. The natural tendency in such a situation is to feel possessive of one's spouse. Yet, when they experienced those feelings, they were accused of having a demon of jealousy.

The teaching on spiritual connections or spiritual unions quite obviously was not scriptural. It violated the biblical teaching on the sanctity of marriage and confused the expression of spirituality with human sexuality. It was a blatant attempt to justify a sensual theology by cloaking it in so-called "revelational teaching." The abusive marital and relational problems that emerged were all conveniently spiritualized by the pastor in a classic example of what sociologists call deviance neutralization, or rationalization.

Scripture tells us, "By their fruit you will recognize them" (Matt. 7:16). From whatever perspective you view it, the fruit of Community Chapel was bad. Family boundaries were broken down, conventional biblical understandings were turned inside out resulting in moral chaos, and hundreds of individuals suffered psychological impairment of indescribable proportions. It is a sobering lesson in what can happen when abusive churches go over the edge.

3

PAST AND PRESENT ABUSIVE CHURCHES ARE NOT NEW

3

PAST AND PRESENT
Abusive Churches
Are Not New

It is tempting to think of extreme authoritarian sects as a symptom of modern intellectual and religious aliments. We live in a complex world where personal security is a rare commodity. Pick up any national paper or magazine and you will find articles on stress, marital problems, substance abuse, and the increase of gang-related violence. Contemporary preachers warn us that materialism and consumerism draw us away from God; we have become an ego-centered society that shuns the simple values and simple faith accepted by citizens one hundred years ago. It is no wonder then that immorality in the church itself is becoming more visible. It is no wonder that people, beset by anxieties and confused by scandal, should find shelter in the more structured environment of an authoritarian church.

In America, which has been a haven for numerous small religious sects, there are important historical precedents for abusive churches. Most sects offered variety rather than aberration, but a few could be categorized as extreme. As with their modern counterparts, they often began with noble aspirations and biblical foundations, but were led astray through human frailty. The whole of church history has indeed been one of conflict and reform. The body of Christ may be one, but Christ's churches are many.

People have always struggled with the same needs—to be accepted by their friends and family, to find their way to God, and to make a contribution to their world. Humanity's fear of loneliness and hope of salvation were no less real to people in the previous century than they are to us today. Unfortunately, there have also always been charismatic figures ready to take advantage of those most afraid and most hopeful.

One nineteenth-century religious community, in particular, has many similarities to modern manifestations. There are other examples of authoritarian abuse but, perhaps, none as intriguing. It is not representative of all turn-of-the-century Protestant sects, but it is a good example of an extremist community based on the near worship of a single man. Frank Sandford's community at Shiloh offers insights into an abusive fringe church from its conception in the late nineteenth century to its "scattering" in 1920.

Shiloh must be understood in perspective. It did not spring from a vacuum. Many of the principles upon which Shiloh was based are rooted in the larger social and religious movements of its day. The nineteenth century was characterized by a restless spirituality that reflected a tumultuous period of history. During the nineteenth century, Americans' perspectives of themselves and the world were altered forever. At the start of the century America was a new country, largely rural and agricultural with an entire continent to explore and subdue. By the close of the century America was a world power fueled by new cities and industry. Rapid urbanization brought a host of new social and economic problems that gradually replaced the nostalgic picture of the rugged pioneer carving out his identity with a plow and rifle, his stalwart family at his side. The church met this challenge of rapid growth, not as a unified body, but as an ever-growing number of denominations and sects. The problem faced then and now remains the same: **which** church shall I join? As Martin Marty has said, "Nowhere in the world and never in history had Christians been divided into so many conflicting groups as in America. Nowhere else were people on pilgrimage forced to make their religious choice from among appeals by more conflicting organizations."[1]

Two concepts dividing Protestantism that were easily used by extremist churches were the ideas of the *kingdom of God* and the *second coming of Christ.* The kingdom of God was a utopian dream that was very easy for the nineteenth century to accept. The hundred years before the first World War were dominated by the belief in humanity's potential to achieve perfection. Popular preachers proclaimed the kingdom of God as an achievable goal for the people of God, a perfect society of committed Christians uniting the world under God's banner. For most, the kingdom of God was a theological concept, not a blueprint for society. It was quickly accepted by the growing numbers of believers who looked at the Second Coming as an event that would occur in the imminent future. The kingdom of God was an idea that transcended traditional churches and transformed humanity into an organized body, subservient to the will of God.[2] The aim was to model the simple faith and lifestyle of the early church, and this was accepted by believers who chose a rigorous communal lifestyle in anticipation of the Second Coming. For followers of Frank Sandford, the kingdom of God was the community of Shiloh on the banks of the Androscoggin River in southern Maine.

A visitor to Shiloh at the turn of the century would have found a large community of men and women dedicated to their work of preparing the world for Christ's return. Almost all members of the Shiloh movement came from traditional Christian backgrounds. They gave up their independence and livelihoods to travel to Shiloh as disciples of Frank Sandford. If one were to look strictly at the surface, Shiloh's achievements were impressive. Beyond Sandford's charismatic ability to demand unswerving respect and obedience from his followers, he had managed to build a large complex of structures, all built and financed by the members of the community. The main building was called Shiloh, after which the movement was named. It was a three-storied, rambling structure resembling a castle complete with turrets, towers, and a large golden dome that shone like a beacon in the sun.

Shiloh was more than just a collection of buildings or followers. It was a testament to one man's faith and authority. The people of Shiloh pledged allegiance to a man to whom God spoke directly, despite clear evidence that this man's version of reality was vastly different from the rest of the world's. Perhaps that was the thing that most drew people into Sandford's world. His reality was different. His call to discipleship challenged one's faith, and by great suffering they were saved. The sacrifices people made of their lives and the lives of their children were willingly made as necessary to please God. Suffering in the proper context has never been considered a hindrance to faith in the Christian church. Often it has been seen as a testament of faith. Shiloh's error was not in denying the flesh, but doing so to satisfy the whims of a man more in love with power than with God.

Frank Sandford, convicted murderer and destined to be the leader of an international revival movement, came from humble beginnings. He was born on October 2, 1862 into a large family whose farm was located in the same region of Maine where he would later bring his congregation. In 1886, after graduating from Bates College, he entered Cobb Divinity School. He left seminary without completing a degree. Sandford sought a more immediate, less academic, and almost mystical knowledge of God, and God spoke to him directly and told him to leave seminary. From then on, Sandford believed that God spoke to him in a clear, quiet voice. This served two purposes. It gave Sandford necessary authority as the chosen spokesman for God, and it gave his important decisions holy sanction.

Sandford married Helen Kinney a few years later and served as a pastor in two New England Baptist churches before God told him to abandon his church and his denomination. While serving as a pastor, he became increasingly interested in the ministry of divine healing and the Second Coming. It became clear to Sandford that not all Christians would belong in the last faithful remnant of believers. At the end of the world, the human race would be divided into servants of the Lord and servants of the Antichrist. No current church or movement could satisfy the rigorous spiritual demands needed to qualify for the last remnant; a new army of God must be formed. Members were welcome from all denominational backgrounds. Non-members would be listed in the roll call of the Antichrist.[3] This apocalyptic or prophetic elitism set the members of this new band, what would eventually become Shiloh, apart from the rest of the world. It gave its members cosmic significance and assurance of salvation. There was no other choice for anyone desiring to be counted in the last remnant.

After leaving the church, Frank and Helen took up the lives of itinerant preachers. Seeking the signs and wonders that were to accompany the return of Christ, Sandford asked to be filled with the Holy Spirit. After being filled, Sandford received another message from God. "He said I need have no responsibility whatever, but simply respond to His movings."[4] Again God had affirmed his spokesman, and at the same time allowed him to put on a peculiar, amoral overcoat. Sandford's responsibility was a key issue at all the Shiloh criminal trials and helped to convict him of manslaughter, kidnapping, and child endangerment. Sandford never denied his deeds, but defended his actions because he was "only following divine orders." For this man, devoid of remorse, guilt, or even compassion, hundreds of parents beat their children, watched them starve, and were even willing to die themselves. To the day he died, Sandford refused to accept any blame or to show any sorrow for one thing that happened to the souls placed in his care.

His renewed zeal and impassioned preaching drew a growing flock of followers. It was the beginning of a movement. As Sandford's ministry was becoming more popular with the people, he became increasingly unpopular with the local churches. There is some justification for the local churches' resentment toward his work. Sandford was luring away members of their own congregations, and he encouraged his followers to break ties with established churches.

The next logical step in Sandford's plan was to create a location where his followers could be trained for missionary work. All contemporary Bible Schools were rejected because they neither studied the "whole Bible" nor possessed the "whole truth." The truth was found only in the teachings of Frank Sandford. The *Holy Ghost and Us Bible School* was founded in October of 1895, and the opening of the school marks the beginning of a recognizable movement, later called Shiloh. The first class numbered less than a dozen. They were all former members of Christian churches, but at Sandford's insistence they were rebaptized, renounced all established denominations, and received the authentic stamp of the Holy Spirit. Students were drawn into the church and remained because of Sandford's personal charisma. David Wiley, who was a member of the group, said, "I was enormously impressed by the magnitude of the man. His presence was powerful, like an electric current in the room."[5]

The Bible School was the core of the Shiloh movement. Dedicated students were being trained to serve as witnesses to the truth. Their lives were devoted to that one purpose. No student or full-time member of Shiloh ever worked or earned a wage. All food, materials, money, land, and buildings were donated by supporters who had been cultivated by Frank. The only teacher was Sandford and the only accepted interpretation of Scripture was his. Shiloh's initial students and members were referred to as "David's Band," a reference to King David's renegade army while he was hiding from Saul. The Bible-school students were being trained to fight and to spread Sandford's vision of the kingdom throughout the world. And they were prepared to suffer persecution and hardship. In the Holy Ghost and Us Bible School the important spiritual foundations of Shiloh were laid down: mystic revelations from God to Sandford, the conviction of being set apart by God for some millennial purpose, the absence of individual thought, and unquestioned obedience at all times and in all things. Having accepted these things, Sandford's followers were willing to do anything.

Shiloh's history as a movement begins in the late 1890s and ends in 1920, roughly twenty-five years. In those twenty-five years the movement had its ups and downs. When things went well for Shilohites, it seemed as if God had really chosen them for a special purpose. People donated money and food, buildings were raised and filled with expensive furniture and carpeting. People ate three good meals a day and their faces glowed with purpose. But this side of Shiloh, prosperous and healthy, was a brief and intermittent period at the beginning of the movement. When there were fewer mouths to feed, the financial burden could be borne by outside supporters. As more and more followers realized that salvation was assured only to full-time members on the hill, the place on the compound where the members lived, the crowding of entire families into the dormitory facilities with no means of support placed a tremendous burden on the community. Simply feeding that many bodies became a major struggle that was lost more than won. In the autumn of 1919, children were sent out to the woods to collect leaves and berries, anything that looked edible. They accepted starvation with a stoic attitude; they hungered because it was God's will that they should hunger. They did nothing to save themselves because God had expressly commanded them not to do so; they were to "live on faith."

Money was usually a problem. Shiloh did not borrow money or purchase even necessary food on credit. Many times the kettles in the kitchen were empty for days before a donation of cornmeal arrived. Members who traveled abroad usually started out with less than five dollars in their pockets. Everything was done in faith. Somehow they managed. Frank could always mysteriously come up with large amounts of cash, seemingly out of thin air.

The Shiloh movement expanded briefly at the turn of the century when several foreign missions were established in England, Alexandria, and Jerusalem. These branches were short-lived and unsuccessful, though missionaries struggled there for many years before being called back. Suffering a growing disenchantment with the daily struggles of Shiloh, Sandford turned his energies to Jerusalem, where Christ would soon return. Along with his most loyal and devoted followers, Sandford left Shiloh, which would experience poverty and persecution while he went on extravagant world cruises aboard his yachts, The Coronet and The Kingdom.

Serious setbacks in Shiloh began in response to the very real threat of extinction through starvation, and when police and welfare investigations uncovered certain abuses permitted and even encouraged by Sandford. All of Shiloh's major struggles stemmed from financial pressure and the rigorous behavior required by Sandford.

Even during times of intense struggle and deprivation, the

people of Shiloh were unswervingly loyal to their leader. An average of four hundred people lived at Shiloh, and every aspect of their personal and family life was subject to Sandford's authority. Although families lived at Shiloh, actual family life was curtailed. Parental authority was diminished as Sandford and his ministers made all final decisions. Members ate together in the huge dining room; there were no cozy family dinners. Later on, one building, Olivet, became the children's dormitory. Even the initiation and dissolution of marriage fell under Sandford's authority. He arranged marriages and performed "separations." At times he splintered families by sending one spouse overseas for years at a time.

Male-female relationships were strictly controlled to preserve propriety. "To avoid appearance of evil," there was no touching of any kind between the sexes. No close friendships were allowed. No child admitted to having a best friend. The leaders encouraged people, even children, to reveal each other's faults. In a world with few material possessions, the most minor flaws became the source of guilt and self-loathing. A young girl confessed to the sin of vanity because she looked in a mirror. Then she was told to fast for three days to atone for her sin. It became a community obsession to root out the most minute bit of evil in their lives with a ruthlessness usually reserved for members of restrictive monastic orders. "It mattered how you acted, how you talked, even how you thought and looked."[6]

One might expect Sandford to have led a life of exemplary behavior. In fact, Shiloh never expected Sandford to withstand the difficulties experienced by the ordinary member. The suffering and denial cheerfully accepted by his followers was seldom shared by their leader. Sandford, Helen, and their five children lived in comfort in separate quarters. They had their own kitchen and cook. Members of Shiloh who were eating only a bowl of cornmeal a day knew that the Sandfords never went hungry. When times were tough on the hill, Sandford found time to travel on his well-provisioned yachts to Jerusalem. A double standard existed, and it remained unquestioned to the end.

The source of Sandford's unquestioned authority was God.

Interpreting God's will was not left to chance since God spoke directly to Sandford. That God often spoke in verses from Scripture helped validate the messages. Frank soon became the anointed messenger of God and declared his power to forgive sins in God's name. "God is here, and the representative of God is here that has power and authority from God to remit your sins. . . . I declare that every one of your sins will be remitted today if you are baptized. . . . If you accept it, you accept 'the counsel of God.' If you reject it, you reject 'the counsel of God.' "[7] Sandford made it very clear that his words were divinely inspired and members would no more question his word than they would question Scripture. His words and decisions became synonymous with God's.

In 1904, the members of Shiloh created a large banner containing a testament of faith, a pledge of allegiance, which all the members signed. The initial tenets would be familiar to most evangelical Christians today, but the last items on the list were unquestionably unorthodox. Those who signed the pledge, every child and adult, agreed that Frank Sandford was a prophet (Elijah), Priest (Melchizedek), and prince (David).[8]

Obedience to Sandford's will was nonnegotiable and absolute. Members were undaunted by suffering as Sandford reminded them that "the strongest character is the one who can suffer the most."[9] Any sign of willfulness or independence was destroyed. The preoccupation with creating an army for Armageddon required soldier-like responses. "It is obey the rules and tactics in the Great War Book [the Bible] or get out, and cease to be a stumbling block to those who are resolved to follow and obey."[10]

For anyone to be disobedient to their superior was to disobey God himself. Outsiders often wondered how people fell in with Sandford's plans so easily. They failed to understand how complete Sandford's hold was over members; he held their very souls in his hand. People obeyed willingly. "Sandford honestly believed that if individual members of Shiloh were each properly adjusted to the mind of God, . . .there would be no barrier to accepting the chain of authority."[11]

One of the keys to enforcing his authority lay in his anger. Although his temper lived alongside a gentle humor, it was formidable when crossed. He was seen many times to slap his wife in public, to throw chairs off the pulpit, and to incite the fellowship into a violent, loud prayer session called "a charge." He even made an example of his own son, John. When John was seven years old, he disobeyed his father. John learned the penalty for disobedience, as did the entire community through his example. Sandford declared that John should be isolated in a room, denied food and water, and then he would be whipped. There was a twist to the whipping—John had to earnestly desire to be beaten. For three days John was in a room, a glass of water torturously placed out of reach on the nightstand, learning to be happy about suffering. Each day he would climb the staircase to his father's prayer room and ask for his whipping, but Frank did not find him happy enough until the third day.

Shiloh doctrine stated that ill health was a sign of disobedience and rebellion. Sandford decided that the children played an important role in the development of disease and he used them as a weapon. "If a child misbehaved, it was as if the parents had directly disobeyed God, and God might punish the parents by punishing or even killing the child."[12] Since children were the source of the problem, ridding them of their sins and wickedness became essential.

Illness was a sign that the soul was sick, and if children were ill it was due not to malnutrition but to their sinful state. Sick children were told "to get right with God" by fasting and praying on their knees for extended periods of time. In some way their sins were causing Shiloh to suffer. Since the children were wayward and disobedient, fasting and being whipped were the ways in which they were punished. The beatings continued day and night. One father beat his young son all evening until someone stopped him at 1:00 A.M. There were rumors of older boys being taken out to the woods and beaten with horsewhips. One mother heard Sandford say that whipping a child was "the schoolmaster to bring them to Christ."

Again and again Sandford told his flock to trust in his

leadership. To question his authority was to bring disharmony into the group. Members accepted Frank's reality as their own. If he had said that Theodore Roosevelt was the Antichrist, they would have believed it. The object of Frank's authority was to break down individual will and self-identity. At various times Sandford laid hands upon the heads of members who exhibited too much individuality and exorcised the demons of independent thinking and reasoning. The only thing that mattered was faith. Thinking accomplished nothing. The "death of self" became a spiritual goal for full members of Shiloh. If Sandford asked them to suffer in the process, they admired him even more for pulling holiness out of them.

There was little privacy in Shiloh and Sandford did not hesitate in becoming involved in peoples' personal relationships. He encouraged Eliza Leger to leave her husband who had recently left the movement. She was torn between obeying Sandford the anointed leader and her duties as a wife to her husband. In a letter to Eliza, Sandford wrote, "The act of your husband is so dastardly...so utterly unscriptural that there is not the slightest reason that he should have the slightest consideration."[13] Engaged and married people who began relationships without Sandford's permission, when he was abroad or, later, imprisoned, were told to "separate" until he had given them their blessings. It was not uncommon to see separated couples walk on the same road without speaking.

As the movement grew, its spiritual elitism became more pronounced. Their physical isolation on the hill was just a part of their separateness from the rest of the world. A visitor to Shiloh would notice immediately that Shilohites were different. They spoke differently. Their clothes were old, simple, and well mended, and their lifestyle certainly was unusual. From the beginning of the Holy Ghost and Us Bible School, David's Band was the spiritual elite. Only the fittest warriors were selected. Frank wrote later that he had to literally scare some people away. The rigors of his community discouraged all but the most worthy. He wanted no ordinary Christians. Shiloh was to be the focal point of the kingdom of God.

When the movement experienced opposition and criticism, their very elitism became a defense against the arrows of the Devil. In 1901 Sandford closed Shiloh's communion and worship services to all but full members. If families opposed their relatives giving all their possessions to Shiloh, the members "must be ready to slash every natural tie—turn their backs on their families, if families should oppose obedience to God."[14] Stanford wrote, "You are actually to *hate*, WITH A PERFECT HATRED, your father, mother, brother, sister, child, and even your own life, in so far as these are not in conformity with the word of God."[15]

Many families did dissolve, marriages broke up, and children abandoned Shiloh only to be disfellowshipped by their parents. There was no higher allegiance than to Sandford, for allegiance to him was allegiance to God. Frank warned his followers:

> First you will be out of joint with the world, then out of joint with the professed Christian world, then out of joint with consecrated people, and then sanctified people, and then people that believe in Divine Healing, and then the Holy Ghost people you know, and THEN you will find a few other people who have gone on alone with God.[16]

One of Sandford's greatest weaknesses as a leader was his lack of compassion. He enjoyed the simple exercise of power and authority. The people at Shiloh rarely were given any meat. They lived mainly on cornmeal. When some members prayed for meat during one of Sandford's trips to Palestine, Sandford arranged for a side of beef to be delivered. He made everyone eat nothing but beef until the entire 1,425 pounds were finished. That much meat, after a vegetarian diet, made everyone sick, but it ended prayers for meat. He seemed willfully ignorant of the pain his followers endured for his sake while living the good life himself.

Even though Shiloh averaged around four hundred people throughout most of its history, not all those who experienced it were happy. A few did rebel. Most were bitter when they left and went to the newspapers with their stories. Some even filed lawsuits against Sandford. Ex-members told stories of physical or psychological manipulation and abuse.

Former members remembered subtle means for disorienting the members. For example, there was no schedule for work or prayer. At any moment during the day or night a loud alarm bell would call members to prayers or to other work. Members worked hard at keeping up the grounds and constructing new buildings. They were hungry, often overworked, and spiritually intimidated. Eliza Leger said she was "metaphysically stoned." She lay prostrate on the floor for many hours while fellow members circled her body shouting and screaming as they accused her of "spiritual lapses."[17] She was then banished to a room for two weeks of fasting.

Sandford interpreted any dissent as the work of Satan. John Douglas was one of Frank's earliest converts and most of Shiloh stood on land donated by John and his family. When John left right after the first building had been raised, after a disagreement over ownership of a small boat, local reporters who were critical of Shiloh, and who had been watching Sandford and his group, picked up the story of Douglas' defection and gave Sandford his first dose of public criticism. Frank answered the papers in his magazine, "[Satan] has used godless editors and reporters to write up the most sensational and glaringly false statements concerning this work...thus poisoning the minds of the people all over the country against God's movement."[18]

Ex-members were called quitters, turncoats, and traitors. At first they simply lost their place in the Lord's roll call, but gradually the act of leaving became an act of disloyalty. Ex-members were not to be spoken to or about. Georgia Sheller was told to have no fellowship with her parents who had left angrily and bitterly. She wrote to her parents, "I am following Elijah, and since you have deserted him I cannot and do not have anything more to do with you."[19] This treatment extended to members of Frank's own family. Two of his daughters, Marguerite and Deborah, left as teenagers. They were both shunned, and Helen was forbidden to answer their letters. It was expected that you would stay with the community, even if it meant leaving your family behind.

To break away from the group required more effort than to

join. After Eliza Leger left she said that "the hypnotic spell began to break as soon as I dared decide that something was wrong with this man. . . . I know that it is a part of that dreadful, subtle snare that some have broken away from, but that holds so many still under its power."[20] Staying was painful, but leaving was even more so. Members were told that to leave was to invite certain punishment and divine retribution. After Albert Field left with his family, he had a family portrait taken in case they should all perish from God's wrath. Leaving also involved some real risk. All possessions were left at Shiloh. People left only with the clothes on their backs. Every member deeded their businesses, family farms, and all other assets to Shiloh to qualify as full members. When they left, they left destitute.

Some were unable to face the real world again and returned to Shiloh. Years of dependence did not make it easy for people to make their own decisions and fend for themselves. Those who did return were shunned, isolated in remote houses until they had earned forgiveness. Merlyn Bartlett left twice. She could not endure the condemnation after her return. When she left the second time, she was followed by Shiloh ministers who rode with her in the train denouncing her to the other passengers as "a whore."

The wrath of God fell not only upon those who dared to leave Shiloh. Parents of children who escaped were punished, and so were those who failed at parental discipline. Those questioning any aspect of the ministry were severely reprimanded and punished. Dissent became synonymous with demon possession. It was a convenient way to bring dissenters back into fellowship. It was easier to blame a demon than to admit you had disagreed. Only a person exorcised could be fully forgiven. More often than not, demonic possession was evident when a man simply thought for himself. Sandford said, "Think clearly as he may. . .he cannot get anything correct . . .there is only one way out, the person has to submit or is sent away in disgrace."[21]

Periods of dissent, grumbling, or restlessness were followed by purges. The threat of being excommunicated and thrown out of the kingdom resulted in a renewal of allegiances. These purges were known as "the sifting-out process" or "cleaning-out time." Sandford was looking for only the "fair, clear, and terrible." The first purge in 1890 was meant to purify the members. The purge was a ruthless examination of character and soul. If you passed the test you were allowed to attend a special service for which you were given a ticket. Members considered the tickets to be beyond price. On the ticket were printed the words "fair," meaning no blemish, "clear," meaning no guile, and "terrible," referring to the face of Satan when he met a child of God. This purge, like the others that followed, was less a spiritual purification process than it was a reindoctrination, a means to solidify Sandford's authority. The purges lasted for weeks, representing long grueling hours of prayer and fasting followed by intense interrogation. Only the submissive and defenseless were accepted.

Sandford interpreted every criticism as a demonic attempt to destroy the kingdom of God. "The malevolence of our detractors only shows that the devil fears the work that we are doing and will take any means to balk us."[22] He did not seem to worry about legal prosecution because God would deliver him from his enemies and detractors. He believed himself to be the prophet Elijah, and as Elijah, he expected to be persecuted and scorned. But he would prevail. Sandford threatened reporters who mocked him, "before long [they] will meet the God of judgment."[23]

Sandford was arrested on January 23, 1904 on charges of manslaughter in the case of Leander Bartlett, and child abuse in the case of John Sandford. The case of John Sandford was over in a single day, February 3rd. Sandford was found guilty of abuse and neglect in requiring his son to fast with neither food nor water for three days. The manslaughter trial began the next morning.

Leander Bartlett had died of diphtheria that January 25th in Bethesda, the Shiloh infirmary. He had come to Shiloh with his mother and sister, and he was a lively and good-natured boy. He was fourteen years old when he died. Leander had fallen suddenly ill in the middle of January. He became so weak that he could not stand and was carried to Bethesda in the middle of the night. It came out at the trial that Leander had received no medical or spiritual help during the next week, the last week of his life. A week after Leander was admitted, Joseph Sutherland was admitted with small pox. Joseph had refused to obey Sandford's order to cover his face while visiting small pox victims. Sandford heard a message from God, "Dead. He said he would hearken unto thee, and he hearkened not."[24] It was revealed on Sunday, January 25 that both Leander and Joseph had died that day. Helen wrote to the overseas missions, "God has been showing His jealousy for David Truth [Sandford]...the curse falling on those who deviate from it in the least degree."[25]

Leander's death was also seen as a punishment as he had confessed before dying that when he became ill he had been planning to run away.

The offenders had been punished. No one was allowed to grieve for Sutherland. Sandford had "separated" Mrs. Sutherland from her husband while he lay dying in Bethesda. He told her that even though he had married them, he wasn't happy about their relationship. While her husband died, she sat in a public chapel listening to Sandford tell her that she was now married to Christ because Joseph had been struck down for spiritual pride and seeking popularity. Mrs. Sutherland never fully recovered from the blow.[26] Leander was buried in the Shiloh cemetery. Where other graves bore loving epitaphs, Leander's bore only a name and a date.

The definition of manslaughter in the trial hinged on the interpretation of death by negligent omission. The prosecution had to prove that Leander was denied care and treatment. The matter of faith healing was really not the central issue. Sandford was convicted because he withheld not only medical treatment, but faith healing as well. Leander, who had planned to run away, was denied a doctor and a minister. Diphtheria at the time was treatable and almost one hundred percent curable if an antitoxin was given at the onset of the disease. In the end, the jury had to decide if Sandford had withheld faith healing out of spite or ill will, in order to make an example of what would happen to disobedient members. Current and former members took the stand verifying that Leander received no substantial care for the week he was sick before he died. In fact, he had been denied food and water during a seventy-two hour fast. Some testimony was especially damning. "He [Sandford] stretched his hands out before him and said he wouldn't care, or he would like to see. . .his dead corpse before him. . . . He said he couldn't pray for him."[27]

During his court appearances Sandford took a passive role, neither conferring with his attorney nor taking the stand in his own defense. He seemed completely at ease and unperturbed by the possibility of a conviction. The people of Shiloh flocked to the courthouse to watch the proceedings quietly, trying to avoid the reporters who surrounded the building. In less than two hours the jury returned the verdict of guilty.

It took two years and many appeals before the verdict was overturned (the prosecution was not able to prove "culpable indifference"). During those years Sandford became convinced that the Tribulation had begun and if they were to be the refuge in the wilderness, Shiloh needed to be self-sufficient. Shiloh was incorporated as the Kingdom of David. More property was purchased, including dairies and farms. Only a self-sufficient community would be able to ride out the Tribulation. Sandford began asking families to join the movement. People across the nation, eager to be a part of the true church, sold their farms and transferred their assets to the Kingdom. They had been promised farms in Durham purchased by the Kingdom in their names. In fact, only seven of the twenty-two donors arrived to find land in their names.

Sandford's second trial followed the disastrous voyage of 1911. Sandford had felt it difficult to deal with the problems at Shiloh and retreated to his yacht, The Coronet. He selected the best and most loyal members of Shiloh to serve as his crew. After a long, tedious voyage around the globe in an overcrowded boat, Sandford at last returned home to the Atlantic coast. He was wanted by the police on a kidnapping charge made by Florence Whittaker, who had been detained against her will on board one of the Kingdom yachts before being rescued by the local Sheriff. Although most of the passengers had not known, Sandford was on the run from the law. The Coronet shuttled up and down the coast, across the

Atlantic to Africa, trying to stay in international waters. When supplies of food and water were almost gone, Sandford still refused to land, even in a foreign port. The boat, built to house a maximum of thirty people, was being occupied by more than fifty. Some crew members and passengers fell ill, and some died. For the last few months the passengers survived on biscuits and rainwater rations. The boat had to be pumped twenty-four hours a day. Men became so weak that they could not climb up on deck. The men, women, and children aboard lost their will to live. The constant storms broke the schooner's masts, and it became impossible to keep warm and dry in the middle of the storm-tossed North Atlantic. The passengers and crew began to lose their teeth and suffer constant diarrhea. By the time scurvy was suspected, it was too late. Much later, Roland Whittom remarked that he "could not understand how we could have allowed the man to dominate us so."[28] Only when faced with a possible mutiny did Sandford agree to return.

When The Coronet finally limped into a Maine harbor on October 21st, six people had died of scurvy and many more were critically ill. Sandford was immediately arrested for kidnapping, but when inspectors saw the condition of the boat and crew, Sandford was arrested for more serious charges, "that he did unlawfully, knowingly, and willingly allow a ship to proceed on a voyage at sea without sufficient provisions." At his trial he admitted his guilt to the jury but claimed he was only doing what God had ordered. He was sentenced to ten years in the Atlanta Federal Penitentiary. Three years were cut off from his sentence for good behavior.

The final blow to the movement occurred after Sandford returned from prison. He was unhappy with the poverty and listlessness at Shiloh and retreated to Boston in 1919. He became increasingly paranoid, driving in cars with shades pulled down and keeping all the curtains in his house drawn. Despite being abandoned by Sandford, Shiloh still numbered almost four hundred members.

In February 1920 a civil suit was brought against William Hastings, a member of Shiloh, for the custody of six of his eight children who were still living in Shiloh. Their mother had died and her family, along with the two eldest children, sued Hastings for nonsupport. Although Sandford was not a defendant in the trial, this was the case that would finally bring his church down.

On the stand, the Hastings children recounted the poverty they had experienced. Ten-year-old David said he couldn't ever remember having had breakfast before school, although he did have lard on his bread as a Christmas present. His older sister Mary recounted how, because she was too malnourished, she was hidden in the woods when Child Welfare inspectors came. Neighbors testified to feeding starving children. In his testimony William admitted that they did not have enough to eat, but he refused to work for wages as it was against God's law. He was living on faith even if his children starved, indeed, as they had most of their lives. Hastings lost the battle and his children were taken from him.

Shiloh stood at a turning point. Sandford's attorney warned him that other families would use the Hastings case as precedent and that soon most of the children would be taken from Shiloh. God then sent word to Sandford in Boston that it was now acceptable for full-time members to earn a wage. It was a simple thing really, but it destroyed the movement. When men went to work in the mills and farms surrounding Shiloh, the atmosphere of holiness and separateness was removed. The Bible School closed, and in one month the population was down to one hundred members. Members who had listened to Sandford's words finally wondered why God would change his mind on something so pivotal to the movement. If they could earn a wage, they could wait for the Lord's return in more comfortable settings. It was no longer necessary to suffer in order to live the Christian life. The purpose for Shiloh's existence simply evaporated. A short time later Sandford ordered everyone to abandon Shiloh.

Sandford remained a leader of a small group of loyal followers, many of whom had endured through many hardships and tragedies. A small group of believers continues to be known as "The Kingdom." The Shiloh complex has long since disintegrated, but in a few homes Sandford is still revered as a prophet and man of God. Shirley Nelson, whose family history is part of the history of Shiloh, puts the purpose of remembering Shiloh in perspective: "I tell it for all the innocent, for those who. . .are bound to be the victims, destined to fall from the cliffs of someone else's ascent toward the highest and the best."[29]

The story of Shiloh is not unlike other nineteenth century American religious experiments that emerged around a single authoritarian leader. One way to achieve an understanding of current abusive movements is to step back and take a broader, historical perspective. An examination of Sandford's Shiloh reveals amazing parallels to the spiritually abusive groups of today.

The lesson we learn from Frank Sandford is that there is indeed nothing new about "new" Christian movements. Now, as in the past, the spiritual power holders exert strong control-oriented leadership and exercise immense influence in the day-to-day lives of adherents. In the present, like the past, Christian groups claim new divine revelation through inspired prophets or preachers who "receive a word from the Lord" regularly. Like Sandford and his predecessors, today's movements express the conviction they alone are the repository of "truth," or that they have been chosen by God to restore a lost or dormant spiritual vitality. Both groupings share a strong consciousness of persecution; both illustrate attitudes of negativity toward established churches; both view their "spiritual family" as superior to the biological family; and both have exhibited concern about the role and fate of ex-members. In short, the narrative of churches that abuse has important beginnings in our past.

4

AUTHORITY AND POWER ABUSIVE CHURCHES MISUSE SPIRITUAL AUTHORITY

4

AUTHORITY AND POWER
Abusive Churches
Misuse Spiritual Authority

"It took some time for me to adjust after leaving the Church of Bible Understanding. When I first began attending church again and meeting with Pastor Tom, I found it very difficult to relax around him. Sometimes I would cringe and freeze up when seeing him walk down the hall, and Pastor Tom is one of the kindest, most disarming people I know.

"It took a few months for me to relax. Even now, when attending a church service, I may feel like I should be participating in some way, or I may get extremely paranoid, start worrying about my true spiritual condition and dive into an intense self-examination. These experiences have lessened as time has gone by, and I have confidence in God's Word and in my own relationship with the Lord." Thus ends Betty Donald's personal account of her fourteen-year experience with the Church of Bible Understanding (COBU).

Started by Stewart Traill in 1972 as the "Forever Family," the Church of Bible Understanding now numbers approximately one hundred members living in a number of properties in the northeast United States. Membership peaked in 1978, with several houses and nearly a thousand members. Betty, along with thirty other members, left COBU in April of 1989, after a March 4 meeting in which Stewart claimed he had been teaching in error for twenty-five years, and that he had totally omitted grace in all his teaching. He claimed that he was more a victim than those he had deceived. In

75

what appears to be an attempt to control damages, Mr. Traill then went on, in June of the same year, to tell everyone to forget everything they had ever been taught on the topic that one must be perfect to be born again (using 1 John 3:9, "No one who is born of God will continue to sin, because God's seed remains in him; he cannot go on sinning, because he has been born of God"), and that he himself had just been born again in February 1989.

Betty, like all other COBU members, was afraid to do anything without Stewart Traill's stamp of approval. As one of the "Gayle Helpers" (assistants/"slaves" to Traill's second wife), she enjoyed certain privileges that others did not. Yet she was "scared to death of him." A member never felt truly faithful to God "unless Stewart accepted you." This acceptance evidently waxed and waned, depending on how useful one was to Traill's business or how threatened Traill began to feel by the favored one.

Stewart was in complete control of the money in the communal organization. Betty never cashed one of her own paychecks. All money was turned in and no accounting was ever given of where it went. At one point, when appointed to the Board of Directors, she did see that as much money was spent on COBU telephone calls as on the group's ministry in Haiti, where they had a missionary outreach. Traill made sure that all persons handling group accounts had no experience in financial matters. Any questioning of this policy brought immediate confrontation and public humiliation. Additionally, members were required to submit a special request to one of the Special Request Committees if they wanted to purchase a pair of shoes, pants, jacket, or other article of clothing. The committee would determine if the need was justified. During lunch hours and off times, members were expected to solicit donations from individuals and organizations for "the ministry in Haiti."

COBU members staffed a number of businesses, including S & G Cameras, one of Traill's enterprises, and Christian Brothers Carpet Company, a carpet-cleaning business run by nearly all COBU men. Betty, as a Gayle Helper, had signed a Gayle-Helper Contract, and worked in the camera shop. Everything from purchasing stock to attending trade shows to cleaning dishes and bathrooms was done by the Gayle Helpers, usually on a full-time basis with no compensation. Although privileged to live at Traill's $900,000 estate in Princeton, New Jersey, the Gayle Helpers on the camera-show circuit were expected to sleep in their vans. According to Betty, "These women were called gypsies. They would wash their hair in sinks at gas stations, use the pools at hotels they didn't stay at, and change clothes in bathrooms in restaurants where they wouldn't think of eating. They would pack food to take along and would eat in the van. Everything was written off to the church." In addition, Traill would use COBU's Christian Brothers Carpet Company accounts as a personal bank, using funds freely.

The plan was for COBU members to live as in the days of the apostles, with "all things in common." According to Betty, members believed that they had a "higher calling" because of their deep knowledge, especially the deep knowledge of human nature and the Bible. They considered their understanding of human nature unmatched, giving them spiritual eyes to see into others' consciences and thoughts. As a result, COBU members were, as Betty describes them, "extremely self-righteous and puffed up." Stewart would continuously speak to them of his great expectations for them and their future plans.

Although he was unable to reconcile a drop in member-ship of nearly nine hundred in twelve years, he did claim that his new teaching was very near to the true apostles' teaching. "Jesus showed me the secret behind everything." Highly critical of other churches, Traill would call ex-mem-bers "enemies of the Cross," or "losers trying to throw stones at a winner." According to Betty, whenever COBU was in the news, they considered it persecution because "we were truly following the right way and the devil was angry."

Looking back at it now, Betty believes that the communal-living arrangement was one of the main ways that their lives were controlled. Living on one's own was considered less spiritual as well as dangerous—you were asking for trouble by leaving the "sheepfold walls." Not only were members expected to live together, but all men were expected to quit their outside jobs and work in the group's carpet-cleaning business. Failure to do so resulted in a person being mocked, publicly humiliated, and looked down upon. Normal office jobs were seen as "working for Pharoah." Working for Stewart or COBU, on the other hand, was seen as doing God's will so that members could make the most of their talents rather than helping their employers get rich. Thus, even one's working life was controlled and regimented. Betty reports that males who leave the church have a harder time reentering and adjusting to the outside world because so much of their daily life was sheltered and controlled. Not all "sisters" were expected to work in COBU or Traill-related businesses.

As is often the case in abusive churches, family ties were severed. When members were notified that relatives had died, they were told to "let the dead bury their own dead." Members needed approval to visit family. Betty remembers, "There was always an uneasiness after going to visit your family because of the scrutiny you were put through when you returned." It was expected that COBU members would consider one another as family, and Stewart would often ask, "What would have become of you if Jesus hadn't brought you to this fellowship?" The expected response was, "We'd probably be dead."

Implied guilt and Scripture twisting were often used to manipulate members. Mr. Traill would take Scripture out of context in order to make members do what he wanted. "In the abundance of counselors there is safety," and "He who trusts in his own mind is a fool," were two verses that were often directed at a person who didn't agree with others' opinions of what should be done.

Marriage was discouraged to such an extent that no weddings have been held since 1978. However, Traill divorced his first wife and married Gayle in 1977. Betty recalls that Gayle was set up as the example for all women in the church to follow. "She would walk around in the slinkiest outfits that sometimes made many people blush. Stewart would flaunt her in front of the brothers and tell them, 'Look what you could have.'"

It was Traill's custom to hold late-night meetings that would end anywhere from 1:00 A.M. to 5:00 A.M. Members were then expected to work and function normally the next day. Leaving these meetings for any reason whatsoever, including the use of the rest room, was highly discouraged. During these meetings, "catching and pointing out someone else's wrong behavior was how we proved our desire to be with Jesus, because Jesus hated the wrong, but, of course, not the sinner. This always ended up in public verbal executions that would lead to standoffs and long silences until late in the night." Since women, according to Traill, were naturally manipulative, devious, and maneuvering, they were often the targets for these late-night confrontations. Each woman would then, according to Betty, "have the task of apologizing so that everyone would believe her, so that she could be forgiven for whatever horrible crime she had been accused of and keep from being lynched." A ritual was begun in 1988 in which members who needed to "make their behavior right" in front of the group, were required to have four to five witnesses who would vouch for their sincerity. Insincerity led to repeated humiliation and/or being put "out of fellowship."

Stewart, however, was above scrutiny. According to Betty, "Stewart will only accept 'corrective criticism' coming from a 'right spirit.' Of course, he is the judge of 'right spirits' and whether any criticism is truly constructive." Stewart has also complained at meetings that no one ever tells him what they think of him; yet he makes sure no one has such an opportunity. In a classic double bind, Stewart tells his members that rebellion is the ultimate sin so that if you question him, you are charged with rebelling against the truth and that means rebelling against Jesus!

After leaving COBU, Betty described herself as a "basket case." She found herself in a totally new and strange environment with a few friends who had left with her, and filled with feelings of paranoia. "Here you are, thirty years old, single, alone, and ashamed of the way you have been taken advantage of. After having spent fourteen years with COBU, I felt stupid telling my parents that they had been right.

"Trying to adjust, even opening a checking account, was hard. It was like dropping off the moon. After quitting my job without notice, and because of the way I had quit my jobs before, I knew it would be very difficult to get established. I hadn't held a job for more than a year at any one place in the past seven years. I had virtually no stability—physically, emotionally, and barely mentally. I had an interest in going to a church, but I was very suspicious and didn't think they'd ever understand. Unfortunately, due to the lack of understanding on the part of most members of the church and their inability to deal with someone like me, I received what amounted to a pat on the head and a well-intentioned 'that's nice, but now you're out and you have to go on with your life.' After ten years of isolation and indoctrination in which you think, live, eat, and breathe COBU, it doesn't just go away."

Betty's experience with authoritarian leadership is, unfortunately, not unusual for people who have been a part of spiritually abusive groups. Control-oriented leadership is at the core of all such churches. These spiritual power holders become strong role models, and their dogmatic teaching, bold confidence, and arrogant assertiveness become powerful forces of influence. They use their spiritual authority to intimidate the weak and those who consider leaving their flock, as the following letter demonstrates. It was written by Don Barnett to several members of Community Chapel who were contemplating leaving. Not only did the pastor warn the members that they would lose all their friends in the congregation, but he threatened that demons would harass them and that they would lack power with God.

"As your pastor, I warn you that you are headed for the bottom of the sea. . . . God has called you to this assembly to furnish you with that which you need. Do you have His permission to leave this assembly? When you take yourself out of this move of God. . .you are going to go downhill spiritually. . . . When you run from God, you go to the bottom of the sea. . . . You could lose your souls through this. The Devil can take you down, down, down.

I ask you to repent before God. . .follow your pastor, stick with him, stay in the boat and God will forgive you. You are following emotions and reasoning that has been infiltrated by the Devil. . .you are going to lose eternal rewards. You will not be the same. . .you cannot just walk into any church and think you are safe. God won't honor that. He called you here and I am your pastor, no one else. You must follow me or you will answer to God."

A former associate of Don Barnett describes his style of leadership: "He's ousted everyone who has taken exception to his teaching. He's been a very autocratic leader. Even though he says he allows differences of thought on issues, it's very difficult for him, really, to allow his leaders to view things differently than he does. He'll say from the pulpit that he does, but he'll tell you in person that it's his God-given duty to revise your thinking."

Pastor Phil Aguilar of Set Free Christian Fellowship has been known to say, "You need to trust God through me; I know what's best for you." That same attitude was communicated in one of his sermons when he was discussing his own responsibility as shepherd of Set Free: "People in this church, don't you say anything about each other. I can say anything I want. I can call you anything I want because I have the responsibility and the accountability according to God's Word for each and every one of you. I can say what I want. 'Well, if you can say it, I can say it.' Well, no, you don't know the scriptures. You don't have that responsibility and accountability; I do. So when I get in your face, receive it from the Lord or let your tail wag and go home and cry. Go try and find a TV pastor so that you can turn him on and off anytime you want."

Unhealthy, authoritarian leadership encourages people to place their pastors on pedestals. This is illustrated by the comments of one ex-member of a church located in a major midwestern city. "Little by little this man became the standard by which we all sought to live. The wisdom that poured forth from his lips left us in awe." An ex-member of an east-coast fringe group commented that her tiny church was believed to be the full expression of God and had the mind of Christ. "When the leadership said something, it was taken very seriously as the absolute truth. I was part of what I totally believed was a sold out, godly, and committed church. However, after I left the church, my life was totally shattered."

Evan and his family had a shattering experience as members of the Church of the Great Shepherd, a largely Asian-American congregation located in the greater Los Angeles area. Here is their story.

In a scene reminiscent of a spy thriller, Evan agreed to take his two children to meet with his estranged wife, Stacy, at a neutral location, hopefully secure against any attempts by her to kidnap the children. Evan was to be accompanied by Doug, one of the brothers from the Shepherd's Training Center. Stacy was to be accompanied by Doug's ex-wife, Sandy, and the two Tong brothers, Dirk and Denny, all of whom had been kidnapped and deprogrammed by the mysterious Hill Spaniels within the past three months. Evan was worried about a kidnapping attempt and the inevitable tortuous and abusive deprogramming process of which he had been repeatedly warned by the leader of the Church of the Great Shepherd and the Shepherd's Training Center's (STC), Mrs. Jean Chao Liang. They agreed that Evan's parents' house, three hours from Los Angeles, would be the meeting spot the next day.

Evan, with his two children Kelsey and Janna, and Doug, left at 2:00 A.M. the next morning in order to have the opportunity to scout the area of Evan's parents' home for signs of Mr. Spaniel's white panel van. They were armed with anointed prayer, on guard against evil spirits of deception and lust, and under instructions to manipulate their wives with specific songs during a time of worship in order to bring them back and into submission to the "Body."

The meeting took place during the late morning. Evan's parents watched the children, whom they had only been able to meet briefly twice before. The two women were not swayed by the manipulative "worship," but began speaking to their husbands about what they had all experienced in the Shepherd's Training Center in light of the Scripture: would Jesus ever force a couple to divorce because one partner was against communal living? Would Jesus send a brother out onto the streets of East Los Angeles, or drug-ridden Northwest Pasadena, for weeks without money or even a jacket in order to teach him to repent of alleged sins? Is there any sin in the Bible called "reaction" or "identity"? Would Jesus use a spatula to force food down a six-month-old's throat in order to teach her submission to authority? Would Jesus ever berate a follower into performing lewd acts in front of him in order to show that individual how depraved he is and to "free" him from a lustful or homosexual spirit? Would Jesus ever tell a married couple how and when to have sex?

After discussing the bare facts, looking at the Scriptures (not someone else's interpretations in light of "context"), and having a few hours away from the thought-reforming influence of the communal group, Evan and Doug realized the deception they had been under and the fact that the Scriptures had been twisted in order to get them and the other members of the STC to submit to Jean Liang's wishes. The anger and horror over lost years, and, in the case of Doug and Sandy, lost marriage, did not set in for a couple of days.

Thus began the end of over five years of what was sincerely believed to be "ministry" in the name of God. When Doug and Evan did not return to the STC, and when outside pressures became too intense, Mrs. Liang began sending individuals back to their parents' homes for a cooling off period in order to placate parents and minimize damages to the group. According to former members, they were supposed to return to the STC when the situation was not so volatile. Meanwhile, Hill Spaniels was working with the recent former members, meeting them as they arrived at their parents' home. Each, in turn, was freed from the effects of the thought-reform process by a discussion of the facts and Scripture. Within the month, the Shepherd's Training Center had been reduced to little more than Jean Liang's family of seven.

The Church of the Great Shepherd began in 1985 under the leadership of Stephen Liang, Jean's husband, Doug Yasui, and Roy Chan, all graduates of a well-known evangelical seminary. It began under the name of Asian American Grace and Faith Church, a non-denominational, independent church with an emphasis on worship, an openness to the gifts of the Holy Spirit, and an increased recognition of the place of women in the church. Within a year, Sunday attendance rose to one hundred and fifty, and the church enjoyed a growing reputation as an exciting, charismatic outreach to young adult and college-aged Asian-American Christians.

The next year the name was changed to Asian American Christ Church and Mrs. Liang began preaching occasionally as well as directing the high-school fellowship. The tone began to change, with greater and greater emphasis on absolute obedience to God (through obedience to the leaders God has placed over his sheep). A new emphasis was also placed on the importance of spiritual authority, tithing, and ministry to the poor. Attendance began falling. Mrs. Liang, after facing much opposition, was successful in having herself ordained in a formal service officiated by her father and a local Vineyard pastor.

By this time, an "unintentional community" had begun at the Liang's household, composed of the Liang family and persons interested in communal living (based upon Acts chapters 2 and 4) or doing seminary internships through the church, or simply needing a place to stay. The active life of the church was moved to the Liang household, with Jean taking greater and greater part in the ongoing work of the ministry.

During this time, Stephen Liang began undergoing a period of "spiritual discipline"; God was supposedly bringing him to account for his lack of love and concern for his wife and five children. This discipline, administered by Jean and another "shepherd," consisted of removal from all ministry, public humiliation, and a separation of Stephen from any relationship with his family, particularly Jean. By the time this period was over, Jean was the effective head of the church and the community. Stephen, reportedly by his own choice, no longer slept with his wife, nor was he involved in any outward ministry of preaching, counseling, or teaching. He was relegated to administrative duties. Stephen also began Shepherd's Services, a carpet-cleaning and home-repair business.

By 1988, the church had been reduced to approximately thirty-five persons and services were held at the communal house, rather than at a rented church building. The group's name was changed to Church of the Great Shepherd, and the community had become a legal entity as the Shepherd's Training Center. Jean Liang was now the single shepherd of the STC, having either forced out or disciplined all other potential leaders in the group.

As the head of the STC, Mrs. Liang dictated every aspect of life, whether spiritual, physical, or relational. Doug and Sandy's divorce came about through a twisting of Matthew 5:27-30. Although neither had committed adultery, because of Sandy's reticence to move into the STC, Doug was told that she was causing him to stumble. He must cut her off as he would cut off his hand, so that he might at least enter heaven maimed. Even after they moved into the commune, they were forced to divorce. Doug spent months on the street and was labeled a "pervert" by the leadership. He would be brought back periodically to see if he was sufficiently "repentant." If not, he was turned out again.

Members shared a common purse, with Stephen Liang as head treasurer under Jean's direction. Numerous questionable expenses for the community, and especially for the Liangs, were considered "ministry" write-offs and attached to the tax-exempt church account. Monies were regularly shifted from one account to another. Jean reviewed the accounts and set financial goals for the STC. No money was released without a voucher.

Evan and Stacy's two daughters almost died as a result of Jean Liang's influence, the oldest from being force-fed at six months and routinely beaten, the youngest because of premature birth due to Stacy's being overworked in the communal house. In addition, Roy and Mandy Chan's young son and daughter were severely abused, being regularly beaten or shaken for such offenses as wetting, crying, not keeping their eyes closed, or falling asleep. After a severe shaking of their three-month-old daughter, Jean said that it would be better for her to grow up submissive and retarded than intelligent and rebellious. At the time of this writing, the oldest child is approaching his third birthday.

The bonding of mothers and children was seen as a great sin. Jean regularly separated nursing mothers and their infants, even going so far as to take them from the breast, saying, "You are tying your child to yourself and not to the Lord." This "tying" supposedly endangered the child's salvation. However, former members state that Mrs. Liang's five children are strongly bonded to their mother, but have little respect for their father. Husbands and wives were also separated for long periods. Their relationships supposedly were impure and ungodly, based upon lust and manipulation.

Public times of confrontation, confession, and repentance were common, lasting anywhere from four to twenty hours. These sessions usually took place at night. The airing of the most intimate details of one's life was seen as opening the way for God to take one deeper into the spiritual life. All participants were victimized because of their idealism and desire to more fully serve and love God. These intimate details, including those related to one's sexual behavior, were brought up over and over again to produce feelings of deep guilt. "It amounted to spiritual blackmail," states Evan. Many persons were labeled as homosexuals and were required to write letters to old associates confessing this "sin." Old "sins" were never forgotten nor forgiven.

Also branded as sin was "introspection"—a term given negative connotations by the group, but that in reality meant using one's mind to think critically and being open to the warnings of the Holy Spirit. Members were required to put aside all that they had ever been taught, seek a new salvation experience, and receive the "truth" in one's "gut" (spirit) without the impure filterings of intellect and reflection.

Ties with family and outside friends were severed or severely limited and monitored. It was said that "spirit is thicker than blood." In other words, one's spiritual family, with whom one shared the same calling and vision, was more important than one's natural or biological family.

Eventually, Mrs. Liang was successful in nearly erasing every member's sense of autonomy and personal identity. Members dressed alike, carried the same Bible, the same bag, wore the same glasses, and had the same hairstyles—all for the sake of the "unity of the Body." Any personal belongings of sentimental value were labeled as idolatrous and either thrown away (as in the case of Doug and Sandy's wedding rings), sold very cheaply, or given to the "poor." Interestingly, Mrs. Liang retained many of her personal belongings, and unlike other members, carried a leather bound Bible, a leather organizer, and wore jewelry. It was believed that she was no longer subject to vanity and pride and thus such things were not "idols" in her life. Her children also retained their personal belongings, their own hairstyles, and they received the best clothing and privileges. They were rarely disciplined or required to participate in the work of maintaining the household, a task that was seen as "learning servanthood" and regularly took till 1:00 A.M. every day.

These and many other inequities and atrocities, so easily recognized by the uninitiated, seemed completely justified behaviors to the members of STC because of the influence of Mrs. Liang's spiritual thought-reform program. In obedience to what they presumed was God's will, they obeyed their shepherd without question.

Evan and Stacy are slowly getting their lives back in order. They started with $23.00 in the bank, thousands of dollars of debt to the hospital for Janna's premature birth, and two toddlers whom they barely knew. Nearly everything else was lost to the STC and Jean Liang. They have repeatedly asked themselves, "How could we have gotten involved in such a fiasco?" Both are college educated, Evan only one year away from a Ph.D. degree. Both had been heavily involved in evangelical campus and camp ministries.

As is the case with most former members of abusive churches, they have had to deal with guilt over leaving the group. People who left were said to have committed the sin of blasphemy. Compounding that is the guilt over having joined in the first place and allowing themselves and their children to be so terribly abused.

On looking back, both Evan and Stacy understand the vulnerable position they were in upon joining the STC. They had lost much of the connectedness they had known during their college-ministry years, and were looking for significant relationships. Unfortunately, they and their closest friends were sucked into the group. They were also at major crossroads in terms of career and family. Evan's career was just beginning to take off; they had been married three years and were struggling through normal marriage adjustments, as well as considering having a family; they had just bought their first home and were having major difficulties with the builder; and they were beginning to learn that their early idealism and zeal for God were not easily reconciled in a world full of conflict and doubt. The STC offered a place of definite black-and-white answers, a haven from doubt, a place where idealism for God could flourish, an opportunity for relationships deeper than they had ever known, and an outlet where their desire to love and serve God could be fully expressed. Unfortunately, such an ideal place does not exist in the real world.

As of this writing, only one young man remains under Jean Chao Liang's influence in the Shepherd's Training Center. Other former members have either gone back to their parents' homes or set out on their own to reestablish their lives. Mrs. Liang's promise to reestablish members upon dissolution of the group by selling the communal house has yet to be realized.

Speaking of Jean Liang, Evan says: "She never claimed to be God, only that she had a special calling and relationship with him. She never claimed to be a prophet or apostle, yet acted with that authority and rarely expressed doubt." According to former members, Jean Chao Liang has yet to acknowledge the devastation she has brought to their lives, and may even believe that she is being persecuted for righteousness' sake. On chance meetings with ex-members on the street, she exhorts them to "Go on with the Lord."

Jesus Christ is to be our ultimate role model and our only Shepherd. Jesus refers to himself as the Good Shepherd (John 10:11). A good shepherd leads rather than controls his flock. I have talked to many former members of what is commonly referred to as "the shepherding movement," and they all share the opinion of one man who said, "If your shepherd said jump, your only response was, 'how high?'" It is indeed ironic that an honorable biblical concept like shepherding has taken on such distorted and abusive meanings in some Christian circles.

Pastor Phil Aguilar views himself as the unquestioned leader of his Set Free flock. Sometimes "shepherds" see their umbrella of oversight extending to the most mundane of life experiences. Such was the case when Pastor Phil was watching a high-school football game one evening in Anaheim, California. An ex-member recalls that Aguilar, his assistant pastor, and a rather large number of men were sitting together near the top of the stadium. The game ended and several of the men, along with the assistant pastor, started casually walking down the stadium steps toward the exit. Pastor Phil suddenly called out to them, "Don't follow Aaron, follow Moses!" The little group had to return to where Phil was sitting and stand there for about fifteen minutes before *he* led them out.

Authoritarian pastors frequently use militaristic imagery to illustrate their strict systems of authority and discipline. In 1986 Pastor Don Barnett sermonized about his spiritual soldiers doing the will of the heavenly commander. He made it clear, however, that he was their earthly commander-in-chief.

> "I have always wanted an army under me that would do what I ask—just like that. Not for me. A general never fights for himself; he fights for his nation. He fights for the commander of the state. . . . I don't want to be eulogized. I don't want to be lifted up. . . . But I am the commander of this army.
>
> "I'm willing to lay on the ground in my sleeping roll with the rest of the troops; I don't need an officer's tent. But I'm telling you—and I want you to hear me—and I know I speak not just after the manner of men, but I know that I speak from the Spirit of the Lord when I say, even as Jesus wanted those to imitate him and follow him carefully, and the Apostle Paul also, that I am not wrong in asking that of this congregation.
>
> "We're going through a battle, and you're going to see that those who have brought themselves to the place of discipline and submission, who are really and truly behind their pastor, are going to be the people who are behind God. . . . Those who will not submit will be on the second team, and they probably will be split off eventually. . . . I am asking for a new submission to your pastor. . . . I'm asking that you hear what he's saying and do it. . . . I know that God wants you to do

what I ask you to do, and I know that if you don't, you are going against God himself."

Abuse of the shepherding or discipleship principle is certainly not new. It began in the first century church. In Acts 20:30, 31, Paul the apostle warns that "Even from your own number men will arise and distort the truth in order to draw away disciples after them. So be on your guard!"

5

MANIPULATION AND CONTROL
ABUSIVE CHURCHES
USE FEAR, GUILT,
AND THREATS

5

MANIPULATION AND CONTROL
Abusive Churches Use Fear, Guilt, and Threats

Tom Brown's story of his involvement in the Korea-based University Bible Fellowship (UBF) typifies the victimization of young, idealistic college students on campuses across the country. In their intense desire to seek and serve the true God, they are taken advantage of by sometimes sincere individuals who exploit their ideals to achieve personal goals and fulfillment. Fortunately for Tom, he was not left with a "shipwrecked faith" as so many others have been.

Tom's involvement with UBF began in 1979, during his junior year at Northwestern University. His fraternity roommate of the previous year had been studying with UBF missionary "Sweety" Rhee. When the roommate did not return to school, Sweety turned her attention to Tom. Although at first he hesitated to accept her invitation to attend a UBF worship service, Tom felt that God may have been answering his prayer for a good Bible study to attend. So he accepted the invitation. He was impressed by the earnestness that UBF members displayed, as well as their spiritual intensity, which he found very refreshing. Most of the congregation happened to be Korean missionaries who had come to evangelize on American college campuses.

During his years at Northwestern, Tom had been struggling to grow as a Christian and sincerely desired to find a Bible study in which he could participate and minister to other college students like himself. UBF seemed to be an answer to prayer. Sweety "took very good care" of Tom

during this initial phase, teaching him to write "sogams"—
personal confessions based on Bible passages selected by
the leader—calling him every week, walking him home, and
buying him dinner.

Tom now realizes that he was "love bombed" by Sweety
during this phase, particularly since Sweety was derogative-
ly known as a "no-sheep missionary" among the other UBF
Korean staff. Tom was her only student in an organization
where individually teaching the Bible to many students is
the chief goal. Along with the "love bombing" came initial
subtle manipulations of Tom's time and behavior, as well as
mystical stories of God's providence and judgment toward
the Fellowship. All of this left a deep impression on Tom.

Over time, Sweety learned all about Tom, including his
desire to earn a Ph.D. degree and become a nationally
recognized expert in his field of study. It was at this point
that "Sweety told me that I should give up my own plans
because they were a result of sinful selfishness. She said that
I should serve Jesus instead." Having set the barb of guilt,
Sweety waited until Tom "made the decision to cut off my
own future direction and wait for God's new direction for my
life." Tom suffered a good deal due to that drastic decision.
"Sometimes I cried because of my sense of loss and
frustration."

After his first four months with UBF, Tom met the leader,
Samuel Lee, a short man who spoke broken English. Lee
began doing things that made Tom feel special. In turn, Tom
responded to the attention and recognition, and, for the
group's Spring Conference of 1980, he was asked by Lee to
deliver a message. At this point, Tom's intense indoctrination began.

"Message training" is one of the ways UBF leaders "help"
students to deepen their commitment to the group. Tom
began by studying 1 Corinthians 15 with Samuel Lee. He
was required to memorize and recite the passage for Lee
each time they met. Tom was then to write his own message
on the passage using Lee's previously written message as a
guide. After several revisions, essentially Tom had Samuel
Lee's own message to deliver at the Spring Conference. The
point was that he had had the opportunity to "struggle with

the Word of God and learn from Samuel Lee" as all the Korean missionaries already knew. What Tom and the other Americans did not know at the time was that the Korean missionaries considered Americans to be spiritually inferior to them. "Many of the Korean UBF members call Korea 'Mt. Zion' and refer to non-Koreans as 'Gentiles.'"

As Tom acknowledges, his behavior and perceptions were already changing by the time of the conference. He had manipulated a number of his friends to attend, and, when one balked at the registration fee, Tom told him that payment was a sign of his "commitment to God" and a measure of his "spiritual desire." By the end of the conference, Tom was praying that God would establish him as a Bible teacher for American college students, all past aspirations of doctoral work having been put aside as fleshly, human pride.

Further indoctrination was carried out when Tom and several other American UBF students were invited by Lee to accompany him on his annual "world mission report" journey to Korea. Tom began preparing on his own for the trip by sleeping on the floor, knowing that Koreans did not sleep in beds. He was quite disappointed when Lee and his entourage stayed in hotels—and slept on the beds. He was also instructed to write an autobiography of his life, which would be the basis for the testimony he would give in Korea.

Although his parents were terribly concerned about his making the trip, given the civil unrest in Korea at the time, Tom put aside their fears as evidence of their lack of faith. During the flight and the first day after their arrival, Lee made the students share their autobiographies, after which he would comment about their characters and basic problems. They were then told to condense their writings down to a six-page testimony. It was at this point that Lee began comparing Tom to the apostle Paul; hence one of Tom's UBF nicknames, Tom Paul.

While in Korea, Lee focused his attention on Tom's "training." He made Tom team leader over the other students, encouraged him to focus more on the other students than on his own testimony, and yet continually had him revise and rewrite his testimony, which by this time was retitled, "True Greatness." Tom explains the point of the title: "I had lived my life up to this time seeking human greatness for myself. My decision now was to live as a great servant of God like the apostle Paul."

Lee also began to drive wedges between Tom and his parents, telling Tom that they didn't want him to become a man of God but only a dutiful son. By the end of the journey, Tom had a great vision to become the apostle Paul for the 21st century—through UBF, of course.

Upon returning to Illinois, Tom commuted one hundred miles each day to minister to his sheep in Chicago. Because it was summer break, he lived at home with his parents and worked for his father, but was committing all of his extra time to UBF and the Summer Conference. Sweety put great pressure on him to leave his home to minister full-time in Chicago, and, after a few weeks, he told his parents that he was leaving. His parents, not understanding the power of UBF influence on Tom, spoke to him about his responsibility to make money for his senior year. After Tom responded that he must also do the work of God, his father gave him an ultimatum. Tom packed and left the next day, fully believing that to stay would mean going against God's will. He reasoned that this was part of the persecution one must expect when serving God. Further, his action insured that his "human relationship" with his parents was severed. As Tom says, "Now I was only a servant of God."

After his move, Tom suffered a great deal over his emotional separation from his family. Several of the women missionaries at the UBF center consoled him. According to Tom, many male students in UBF develop a kind of maternal dependency on the women missionaries, related perhaps to the sexually repressive atmosphere of the organization.

He also began to have an attraction for Lee's teenaged daughter, Sarah. At this point, another form of spiritual discipline became an integral part of Tom's indoctrination. "Sweety hit the roof. She harshly rebuked me over and over for my 'sinful desires' for Sarah. Whenever I opened my mouth to protest, she rebuked me more." This response, according to UBF philosophy, was actually demonstrating love for the American students who were lost in their "fleshly desires." Sweety was eventually rebuked—by Samuel Lee—for badgering and rebuking Sarah.

Tom, not able to control his feelings for Sarah, entered into a pit of guilt, shame, and depression. Sweety continued to berate him. He became physically ill. Lee entered into "no-mercy message training" with him. He was given the passage Mark 8:27-38, on Peter's confession of Christ, to prepare for the Summer Conference. Tom was required to write and rewrite the message many times. Each time, Lee would rebuke him more and give him additional rewriting directions. As Tom says, "This served to completely break down my ego. After a week of this training, I felt like I was at the bottom of a deep pit of my sins and weaknesses. No one could help me. I felt I had betrayed God in my sinful life. All I had were sins and sinful desires." He was now ready for additional "training."

Preparation for Summer Conference usually reached fever pitch the three weeks prior to the event. It was during these times that extensive spiritual manipulation and indoctrination occurred. Lee would meet nightly with all the UBF staff, accusing some of "playing Satan," and actually saying that he had prayed they would die if they did not repent. He rebuked some, praised others, and made the "no-sheep" missionaries get together to repent, ridiculing the students' personal problems. He led them all in shouting prayers of repentance that sometimes lasted for hours. These prayers, when spoken correctly in a group of people, could communicate a great deal without one's ever having to speak directly and substantively. Lee would often pray, "Our Father, have mercy on Shepherd Tom Paul (Tom's nickname). He has no spirit." That kind of ambiguous prayer left the victim in a state of confusion and guilt, especially, "when you ask God to forgive someone of something of which they are not aware." Tom himself was to use this same technique later on in his "ministry" with UBF.

After struggling a great deal over whether to complete his college studies, Tom decided to finish out his last year. However, since up to this time his parents had supplemented his income, he was now forced to make up the difference by working as a park grounds keeper. This was heavy work for a man of only 121 pounds. It was at this point, after the rigors of the Summer Conference, that Lee entered Tom into "eating training" and "international stomach training." That meant he was forced to eat far beyond his capacity and to "eat all kinds of foods so that I could become a missionary." Lee would make comments about his picky eating habits and encourage Tom to "overcome" himself by eating foods he knew were too much for his digestive system. Although he did gain fifteen pounds, he suffered greatly. "I ate so much food at dinner that my fraternity brothers could not believe it."

Believing that equipment failures at the park were God's message to him about his unbelief in providence—an emphasis on suffering typical of UBF—Tom quit his job and wrote home demanding that his parents support his schooling. His parents did not budge.

In the fall, after completing his "eating training," Tom embarked on "hair training," supposedly to give him a more pleasing appearance. He was given a permanent and was not allowed to cut his hair. He also had it curled before every worship service. According to Tom, "My hair grew longer than everyone in my fraternity except the house hippie." His appearance was further altered by his wearing of suits (the pants of which always had to have belt loops according to Lee—one of Lee's idiosyncratic and unexplainable quirks).

"Voice training" was next, in order to make Tom's speaking voice more powerful, especially since he was beginning to preside over many meetings. Lee would alternately tell Tom after each of these meetings that he "did not have enough spirit" or that he was "grandstanding" and that "he needed to repent." The inner conflict and confusion left Tom baffled—and open to further "training."

At this point, Tom was in his last year of school. He refused to return home for Thanksgiving since it was purely a "human" celebration and not one of God's concerns. He had given up all extracurricular activities and had thrown away his entire collection of classical and Christian music and most of his books, and he sold his guitar. This last sacrifice was the result of his decline into poverty—he needed the money to survive. He was tithing twenty percent of his income (which increased to forty percent upon graduation) and was pledging $50 per month to the UBF world mission offering. Sweety often had to supplement his "offering" because Tom's income was so minimal. Failure to meet the monthly offering resulted in severe rebuke. Tom himself, at Lee's direction, would shout and pound on tables in his rebuke of a student's "bad attitude toward the offering."

In the spring of 1981, his last quarter at Northwestern, Tom moved into an apartment with his UBF sheep, Mark, partly due to perceived persecution on the part of his fraternity brothers, who, at this point, were sure that he was in a cult. Tom also believed that the "spiritual environment" of the fraternity house was too decadent.

Lee began "testing" Tom in different ways to determine the extent of his commitment—and indoctrination. Once, he was told that he was to leave Northwestern to go and pioneer the UBF work at Harvard University. He was ready to go the next day. Lee also would say things in order to see others' reactions and thereby assess their "spiritual condition." At one point, he told a missionary to give Tom his new car. The "test" got to the point of Tom nearly driving away before Lee was satisfied with the missionary's loyalty.

Upon graduation, Tom visited his parents who again debated his involvement in UBF. His mother expressly stated, to no avail, her view that he was in a destructive group. Tom was unaffected by her concern and her emotional distress. "I told her that I did not want their human [as opposed to spiritual] love, and that human love had made me very sick in my soul." The next day he returned to Chicago to begin life as an "intern" in UBF.

The main emphases of UBF intern training are service and learning "faith." In preparing for leadership positions, interns must learn to serve others and to obey their leaders. The training may last several years, and may involve even more severe spiritual and psychological abuse. Tom had heard that interns in Korea may be beaten by their shepherds in order to break them of their stubbornness and independent spirits.

In the United States, during weekly meetings, the Ameri-

can leaders are required to share their sogams on the passage
they had been studying the week before. They use Samuel
Lee's messages as the basis of their sogams. Their "sharing"
gives the Korean leaders an opportunity to "check their
spiritual condition."

By the 1981 Summer Conference, Tom's internship experience had intensified. He was rebuked by Lee as having
"life security" and "marriage" problems, accusations not
hard to understand when one considers that Tom was living
in poverty, often skipping meals, and, because of his
experience with Sarah, afraid to even talk with any young
women. "All through the conference Lee rebuked me and
prayed for me to repent. When I told him 'I am a great
sinner,' he said, 'No, you are only a small sinner.'" Tom
slept only four hours in four days and finally had to have Lee
dictate the message he was to deliver. It took him almost two
weeks to recover from the humiliations he had suffered.

Tom then entered into "driving training" and "humanity
training." Because of a car he received as a result of
someone's UBF-arranged marriage (dating is considered
sinful indulgence and a lack of trust in God for one's future),
he became chauffeur for the Chicago chapter of UBF. This
he found hard to do, but he was told "to do it for the glory of
God." Also, because of his supposed legalistic character and
lack of human compassion, he was told to "listen closely to
many life testimonies and sogams, read books, and see
certain movies." (The "certain movies" were intended to
inform members about society, the nature of people, and so
on. These movies included "Ben Hur," simply because it
was a favorite of the leader, "Ordinary People," and "ET,"
which supposedly depicted the alienation and plight of the
American teenager!) He thus learned to understand people—for the sake of manipulating them.

Tom began finding that he was adopting the same methods
that had been used on him in order to "train" his sheep. He
would make people stay up all night to repent, hit them with
sticks for not remembering passages, force them to run
distances to "restore their spirits," and squash "rebellion" in
the same way that his own abilities to think independently
had been squashed. "At that time, I was working out many of

my personal frustrations on those who were under my authority."

Lee decided to deal with Tom's "marriage problem" once and for all. He forced him to deliver a sogam entitled "Not a Dog but a Shepherd" to the entire congregation of the Spring Conference of 1982. Supposedly, he was "like a dog barking around a hen house." After delivering that message before hundreds, Tom was numb for almost two weeks. "My feelings were totally burned away."

Two weeks after that, Lee allowed Tom to go to Michigan State University as part of the pioneering team (which also included Sweety Rhee and her husband, who had joined Sweety in the USA after living in Korea for some time). Without the "protective environment of Chicago" and no more strong people to depend upon, Tom began to have a difficult time and began losing his direction as a "campus pioneer." The MSU Summer Conference, designed both as a training conference for younger leaders and as an opportunity for evangelism, was "long on rebuking and short on sleep," and Lee dictated another message for him to deliver. Tom began to wonder if he was being used.

Tom got a full-time job as a maintenance man for a group of apartments and worked for two months prior to the beginning of the fall quarter. He gave up full-time campus pioneering for the time being. By the time Spring Conference rolled around, his life had become somewhat smoother, but he had actually run away from the dissonance his doubts had caused, and was again struggling to keep up his "ministry." Samuel Lee then "decided that he should light a fire under me." Tom was told by one of Lee's messengers that "if I did not have seven one-to-one Bible studies each week, I would have to come to Chicago for additional training."

Tom went out every day to invite students to study the Bible with him. After two weeks, he had twelve Bible students. He also was successful in recruiting three women students, unusual in that UBF has proportionately more men than women (the goal being to raise up male leaders). Sweety strongly disapproved, but Tom had declared that "by faith I would be the 'father of all American women.'" And Samuel Lee had approved.

Summer Conference of 1983 was pivotal for Tom. He was to prepare a message on Luke 5:1-11, the calling of the first disciples, and, for the first time, Samuel Lee did not want to check it before delivery. As Tom says, "It was sink or swim." Because of car problems and the need to get visas, he and his passengers arrived almost a day late to the conference site in Canada. Lee was livid. Tom was asked to write a sixty-page sogam of apology for disappointing all those who had prayed so much for him over the last year. Lee told him that "the most important thing was for us as God's servants to participate in God's history. There was no excuse for being late." Tom was told, "You should have left three foreigners behind in a different country and hitchhiked to the conference in order to arrive on time." He wrote all night to prepare his message. Fortunately, Lee thought that he was able to deliver it "with one main point and with spirit." Tom was spared for the final round.

In September, Tom was told by Lee that he should have a new car for his ministry since his old one was out of commission. Lee personally promised him four thousand dollars and UBF would also contribute five hundred dollars. However, he was told to ask his father for an additional four thousand dollars because "a young man like you should have a new car." His parents, of course, refused, saying that UBF should be responsible. After several rounds of pointless negotiation, Tom began to get the idea that he was being tested again. Lee told him, "You are very sharp."

Tom was to use any means available to extract the four thousand dollars from his parents. Lee did not care how it was done. After several attempts, Tom began to realize that "Not only was I beginning to attempt to exert control over my parents, but I was also beginning to actively try to control the students at the MSU chapter. I used my position and the Bible to get them to make 'decisions of faith' that would conform them to the image of a servant of God that I held. I even began to rewrite messages that students were to deliver, just as Samuel Lee had rewritten mine. Those students who accepted my direction in writing were 'good.'

Those who did not were 'rebellious.' " Tom had become a little Samuel Lee, and he was appalled.

On April 1, 1984, after four years in Samuel Lee's University Bible Fellowship, Tom was convinced to leave through the efforts of his parents and several other concerned persons. He says, "I give thanks to my parents for the best April Fool's joke of my entire life."

———————•◆•———————

Spiritually abusive groups routinely use guilt, fear, and intimidation as effective means for controlling their members. In my opinion, the leaders consciously foster an unhealthy form of dependency, spiritually and interpersonally, by focusing on themes of submission, loyalty, and obedience to those in authority. In all totalitarian environments, dependency is necessary for subjugation. Jerry Mac-Donald, a student of autocratic religious movements, notes that authoritarian religious groups manipulate "rewards, punishments, and experiences to systematically sever from members their past support systems, which include their own powers of independent and rational thinking, their ability to test, define, and evaluate, as well as their ability to freely interact with others about their experiences. These internal support systems are replaced with exterior support systems under the control of the leaders."[1]

One of the areas in which manipulation is exercised in a number of the groups discussed in this book is dating and marriage. Young people who were members of Maranatha Christian Ministries, also known as Maranatha Christian Churches (MCM), including the former Miss America, Debbye Turner, were not permitted to date. As a result of a so-called "dating revelation" received by the leadership, MCM discourages dating practices and cites extreme examples of sexual misconduct in the collegiate subculture (including Christian college students) to justify its stance. Instead, members were told to focus on serving God and then he would bring a mate into their lives. An ex-member of MCM comments: "The doctrine is put into practice by church members submitting the names of other church members whom they feel God may be leading them to as potential mates, and if the leadership confirms the name submitted, you wait on God to speak to the other person. If God speaks to that other person, he or she will submit your name to the church leadership and you will get married."

Pastor Phil Aguilar also does not permit dating. A woman who had been a member of Set Free Christian Fellowship from its inception, gives this account of her daughter's pairing. "In the fall of 1989, my daughter expressed an interest in a young man, and the young man was instructed by Phil to propose to my daughter. She accepted. Of course, they never dated. Phil planned the entire wedding, changing the date several times. They were finally married about six weeks after the proposal.

"Prior to my daughter's wedding, she was advised to quit college and her job. When I questioned Phil, I was simply told that they wanted to see how obedient she would be." When the mother asked her son-in-law-to-be why the daughter needed to quit school, she was told, ". . .the only things we need to know are what Pastor Phil tells us."

Pastor Phil demonstrated his need to control in the case of his own son's wedding. The bride's parents state that "Phil transformed what should have been the beauty and joy of our daughter's marriage into a nightmare, a personal tragedy of such magnitude that only the grace of God could get us through." Phil asserted that the bride's side of the family was to have no input into any of the wedding plans. He explained his thinking by noting that the earthly wedding is a picture of the bride being given over to the Bridegroom. Therefore, since the Bridegroom in Scripture is a reference to Christ, who is the Head of all things, it is the earthly bridegroom (and his father) who is to be the dominating factor in the earthly wedding event.

When the wedding took place, the bride was allowed to be dressed in white, but all attendants wore black. Black balloons and black crepe paper were used as decorations since black is Pastor Phil's favorite color. The ceremony was performed in a black asphalt parking lot.

Traditional evangelical churches value and respect individual differences. For the most part, they encourage people to become unique persons in their own right, not mere photocopies of someone else. Authoritarian, manipulative fringe groups, on the other hand, encourage clones and promote cookie-cutter life-styles. Flavil Yeakley, in his book *The Discipling Dilemma*, suggests that such groups value conformity, not diversity. "They tend to make people over after the image of a group leader, the group norm, or what the group regards as the ideal personality. . . . They are made to feel guilty for being what they are and inferior for not being what the group wants them to be."[2]

Yeakley discovered in his research that the Boston Church of Christ (also known as the Boston Movement) was

> producing in its members the very same pattern of unhealthy personality change that is observed in studies of well-known manipulative sects. The data. . .prove that there is a group dynamic operating in that congregation that influences members to change their personalities to conform to the group norm. . . . The Holy Spirit changes people when they become Christians, but not by making us identical in psychological type. The growth that comes from the Holy Spirit produces a body with many different members that perform many different functions in many different ways.[3]

Another effective control mechanism employed by abusive churches is fear; fear of not measuring up, fear of losing out with God if one leaves the group, and fear of spiritual failure. As one observer colorfully described it, "An incredible environment of fear is created where the hens huddle together within the walls to protect themselves from ravenous wolves, while allowing weasels to guard their chicken coop."[4]

Kim, an ex-member of Maranatha Campus Ministries, clearly recognized one of the tactics of control used in that group—the fear of demons and spirits of deception. "Fear also that if you don't straighten up, God will step on you." Kim's overseer determined that she had a "spirit of deception" that was causing her to be "rebellious." The leadership concluded, "We'll pray over you and cast out this demon." But Kim protested, "Wait a minute. There's no demon; you don't need to pray." "For a moment I was scared. I thought, well, what if there is?"

Several times that night, Kim woke up terrified, scared that she had fallen from grace and was doomed to go to hell. "In my mind, I had equated my salvation with my membership in MCM, even though I had become a Christian two years before I had ever heard of Maranatha."

Kim explains how the process of "deliverance" and "inner healing" was facilitated in Maranatha. "It's the belief of the group that although our sins were dealt with at the cross and our freedom gained at the Resurrection, there is still a big clean-up job that remains. Since all of the saints came out of the world, they are packed full of demonic influences, and are still in the believer until properly dealt with.

"The overseer would usually 'discern' a demon or maybe would receive a revelation about their disciple while in their prayer closet. What was required of the deliveree (the one with the demons), was to pray and think way back to when this particular demon could have gained entry. Sometimes these memories were of the womb when, perhaps, the mother would think something sinful and the demon would enter the unborn child. Ironically, it was usually the overseer who 'remembered' this incident for the disciple.

"Also required was an admission to guilt. The disciple had to confess all the sins that he had done in that particular area in order for the deliverance to work. This usually was accompanied by a barrage of tears and humiliation, since these memories were often painful. The disciple was instructed to then repent from those past sins and renounce the demon. Then the overseer proceeded to cast it out.

"As far as control is concerned, I believe two things are accomplished with deliverance. First, the disciple feels a certain bond to the person confessed to, a pseudo parent whom he can respect as an authority and someone who cares about his personal interest. Secondly, at any future date, the overseer may drag out this dirty laundry to discredit the disciple or make him feel guilty. That happened to me when I was trying to explain my position. My overseer blurted out, 'I hate to bring this up, but. . .' And this was done in a room full of people. My immediate reaction was to curl up and shut up. I had nothing on her but she had a lot on me. That's how it is in Maranatha. The bigger the sheep, the more infallible he is. In short, dirty information about someone travels up the ranks, never down."

Most abusive churches make use of some kind of reporting system or surveillance pattern to insure conformity with group norms. Don Barnett's Community Chapel was very blunt about the mechanics. They put it in the Sunday bulletin. "It is a worldly concept, inspired by the devil, which makes us think it is doing someone a favor to keep their sins hidden from those who are in a position to help. Remember we are our brother's keeper. Please do your friends a favor when you see them making serious mistakes; tell your pastor or an elder so something can be done in time."

An obvious form of control is the teaching or preaching from the pulpit. According to a former member of the shepherding movement, so-called because its members had "shepherds" who required full submission and taught the need for "spiritual authority," these "leaders had the true story of what was going on. Pastors exercised control and manipulation through their sermons. Certain themes came through regularly: covenant, authority, obedience, submission, serving, honoring. . . ."

Another more subtle control mechanism was identified for me by an ex-member of a well-known network of shepherding churches known as the Fellowship of Covenant Ministries and Churches presided over by Charles Simpson ("brother Charles" as he is called). "There were promises on the part of leadership to individual members, like: 'It won't be long before you'll be married.' Well, here it is fifteen years later and I'm still single. My pastor said that some men have the capability of being a captain of tens, but he had a vision of my being a captain of hundreds. That's a promise that's been largely unfulfilled. He told me, 'Wait until you're thirty.' Things were deferred until the age of thirty. I was told I would be a leader by the time I was thirty. So I was really looking forward to being thirty. Well, at age thirty, I was still not a leader."

Control also can be exercised by regulating contacts with

family members and friends from the past. Members who go home to visit friends and relatives are encouraged to keep the visits brief because, "you may lose the vision." When prospective members consider joining Emmaus Christian Fellowship in Colorado, they are told to read a document that spells out the ramifications of their baptismal vow. "Because our lives become intimately intertwined with others in our new family, our lives will profoundly affect our new brothers and sisters. We recognize any disobedience to God's patterns [read: patterns of that group] will necessarily affect others. This makes it necessary that we should submit to God's discipline in our lives not only for our own sake, but for all others as well. . . . God tells us that no earthly relationship should draw us away from our commitment to His covenant Body, thereby bursting through the covering of the Body and making both our own life and the entire Body vulnerable to infection. We must instead be willing to lose our family, our friends, our nation, even our own life if we are to be worthy to be His disciples."

Members of a now defunct Southern California fundamentalist group had to sign a covenant promising to date only Christians, and then only Christians within that particular group. "I will keep these dates 'clean' and refrain from any kissing until six months of dating the same person. I promise God I will not go steady without the approval of those in authority. . . ."

Members of this same group had to "agree to get prior approval from those in authority *before* making any engagement or marriage plans. The timing of any engagement or marriage plans will be coordinated with those in authority." Members also promised God in writing "to try to take vitamin supplements every day" and to refrain from "watching channel 40 on television" (the TBN charismatically oriented channel in Southern California).

6

———

ELITISM AND
PERSECUTION
ABUSIVE CHURCHES
SEE THEMSELVES
AS SPECIAL

6

ELITISM AND
PERSECUTION
Abusive Churches
See Themselves as Special

Barbara Harold was almost twenty-one in the summer of 1988, living in Tempe, Arizona, and attending nursing school in Mesa. While running in the park one night, she was approached by a harmless-looking couple who invited her to attend a "Bible Talk." She declined. The woman pursued her and asked to at least have lunch together so that they might talk. Intrigued, and not having any really close friends, Barbara decided to accept. Within a few weeks, she was attending a regular Bible study with three other girls from the Phoenix Valley Church of Christ, an affiliate of the so-called Boston Movement. Although brought up a Baptist, Barbara had not been to church in four years and was looking for something to which she could belong, to feel a part of. She was looking for friends with whom she could bare her soul and be secure. She joined Phoenix Valley Church of Christ in July of 1988, was baptized in November of that same year, and became an assistant Bible Talk leader by the following June. When she left the church in June of 1990, she was "totally devastated, afraid to be alone, severely depressed, and on the verge of suicide."

While a part of the Phoenix Valley Church of Christ, Barbara's life was very full. After classes and work at the hospital, every evening was filled with activities. Monday and Tuesday she and her friends went "door knocking' (street evangelism) or "blitzed" the local malls. Wednesday they were at church. Thursday was "Bible Talk" night (their

111

term for Bible studies). Friday they had activities with visitors. Saturday was "date night," when all single members of the church were expected to be out on group dates. Sunday night was either Bible Talk leaders' meetings or activities with roommates. Such a schedule left no room for nonchurch activities.

In addition to this full evening schedule, Barbara was told that she must have an hour of quiet time with God each day. Given that she had to be at the hospital each morning at 6:30, Barbara would rise by 4:15 to spend her "quiet time." Invariably, because of the demands of her heavy schedule, she would fall asleep unless someone else was with her. This led to her being called "weak hearted" and lacking in zeal for God by her disciplers (those more mature Christians who supervised her spiritual activity) and the other women in her Bible study. A vicious cycle of emotional highs and guilty depressions resulted.

Her disciplers also told her to quit exercising, something she did four to five times a week, unless she was using it as a means to reach out and share the Gospel. Her regular exercise regimen was seen as being "too self-focused." She was told, "You must live for God's kingdom only." Because she came to believe that her whole family would be lost if she didn't try to convert them (the Boston churches consti-tuted the only "true Church"), Barbara was constantly speaking to them about their salvation. Her family grew tired of the spiritual barrage, as did her old friends, so Barbara ended up moving into an apartment with four other women from the Phoenix Valley Church of Christ.

Although she enjoyed the activities and the pep-rally-like church sermons, Barbara was under constant pressure to be something she wasn't. She was always required to confess sin to her discipler. Not being a very extroverted person, Barbara found it hard to meet the requirement to constantly evangelize. Times with her discipler were like interroga-tions: How many persons did you reach out to today? Barbara's answer was invariably one, two, or none. She was told that because she didn't desire to reach out and witness that Satan was in her, that she didn't have Jesus' heart for the lost, and that she needed to be more like Jesus. Finally, the pressure became so great that she began making up sins to confess so that she would at least have something else to say. She constantly felt guilty.

Members of the Phoenix Valley Church of Christ would compare their "Bible Talks" with the Bible studies of other campus fellowships, and comment on the amount of sexual immorality that *must* be going on in these other groups. Members of their church never went on single dates, but always in groups of four to eight. "Sisters" were never to be alone in a room with "brothers" for more than fifteen minutes. Members required permission to call one another for dates, and, after going out, were grilled by their disciplers about lustful thoughts during those dates. Couples going steady were allowed to hold hands and give one another pecks on the cheek. No solo dating by individual couples was permitted. There was a strong emphasis on getting the brothers married, as "It is not good for the man to be alone (Gen. 2:18)." Consequently, no single sister was ever to be home alone on a Saturday night.

The amount of control exercised over Barbara's life and the life of some of her friends extended to extremely personal levels. Members would quit very good jobs to be "in the ministry" full-time. It was a sign of their dedication to God. Disciplers would tell married couples when and how to have sex, a fact that caused one of Barbara's best friends to leave the church with her husband. Disciplers would require that every single sin, even negative thoughts, be confessed to them. If you "stuffed" bad feelings toward someone down in your heart, that is, if you didn't confess them, you were in sin. This would obviously lead to more sin since a root had already taken hold.

Barbara's last night with the Phoenix Valley Church of Christ was one of severe reprimand and interrogation by the members of her Bible study because of her alleged "stuffing" of bad feelings. The Bible study was not "advancing" (growing in numbers), and she was obviously at fault. What bad feelings and thoughts was she stuffing? Why wasn't she having quality quiet times with the Lord? How many persons was she really reaching out to each day? One by one, each member told her what her shortcomings were.

Yet they all declared their support and love for her, along with their great desire to see her grow.

Barbara asked to move back with her parents that same night. "It was the hardest decision I ever made," she said. She was emotionally unstable, and didn't even know how or what she felt, since she was so used to having someone else tell her that what she was feeling was wrong and of Satan. Her guilt increased, exacerbated by the fact that members contacted her and asked, "How could you allow Satan to harden your heart so much to do this to your friends?" She was told to remember that her heart was "exceedingly deceitful."

That same night she also phoned one of her old disciples, a woman who had been "marked" (shunned) by members of the church for marrying the wrong man. Although one was not supposed to talk to ex-members because they would "try to pull you away," Barbara found it a relief to have someone to talk to. Getting a better perspective by talking things out with her friend, Barbara's resolve not to return grew. Even though at times she felt like she was leaving the "true Church" or turning her back on God and heading for hell, Barbara knew that the "unconditional love" preached by the Boston Movement churches was *very* conditional when it came to ex-members.

Barbara returned to her shared apartment the next morning to gather her things. She ignored the "love bombs" that members and leaders attempted to throw at her—things like invitations to activities, reminders of good times together, and words of encouragement. Somehow she found the strength and courage to walk away from the highly controlling and manipulative environment in which she found herself; she returned home to her family. She had been in the Boston-affiliated Phoenix Valley Church of Christ for two years.

Barbara is concerned for her friends still in the group. Although she knows that she would be indulging in blasphemy in the eyes of the members by calling the Boston movement a destructive group and warning her friends, she realizes that her severe depression, attempted suicide, and sleeping sixteen to eighteen hours a day with no hope for the future are not the results of a ministry centered around Jesus' Gospel of grace. If it was such a wonderful thing that God could lead her and others into such a movement, why must it be of Satan to feel that God has saved her and led her out? She now hopes that others in the Boston Movement will have the strength and courage to question whether they really are right in their convictions, whether God is truly blessing their ministry, and whether they really do belong to the only "true church" on earth.

Barbara knows that one day she will be seeking God and wanting to know the truth again. She believes that God himself will lead her to the right place. But right now she is burned out on church and she knows she is not ready to get involved in *any* kind of church. After twelve weeks of therapy, Barbara is now just beginning to make simple decisions on her own and is attempting to make a normal life for herself.

———————◆———————

The Boston Movement, earlier known as the "Crossroads Movement" and "Multiplying Ministries," had its origins in the Crossroads Church of Christ in Gainesville, Florida, under the leadership of Pastor Chuck Lucas. He stressed personal discipleship training, a variant of the shepherding philosophy so popular during the 1970s. This philosophy stressed the need for every believer to have a "covering" in the Lord, a delegated authority who must be unconditionally obeyed and consulted for even the most personal decisions. One of Lucas' own disciples, Kip McKean, became pastor of a small Church of Christ in Lexington, Massachusetts, in 1979 and transformed a group of less than one hundred members into a thriving congregation worshiping on Sundays in Boston Garden, home of the Celtics. It has been under the leadership and influence of this young evangelist that the Boston Church of Christ has developed into what one observer calls the "Jerusalem" of one of the most controversial and most publicized of the authoritarian movements discussed in this book.

Unlike the mainline Churches of Christ (which have

distanced themselves from this rapidly growing offshoot), the congregations affiliated with the Boston Movement answer to their mother church in Boston. The doctrinal areas that have caused most controversy are those dealing with authority, discipling, baptism, autonomy of congregations, and the role of the leadership, especially the leadership of Kip McKean.

Central to the Boston Movement's belief system is its view of authority. The leaders have justified the use of abusive authority in order to follow Jesus. They demand submission even if the leaders are sinful and un-Christlike. Here are examples of statements made by various Boston leaders that illustrate their position:

> Often we are afraid to submit to authority because it might be abusive. Jesus was not afraid of abusive authority; he was even willing to submit and obey authority that was abusive (Philippians 2:6-11; Matthew 27:11-50). . . . When we trust God, we do not have to be afraid of abusive authority. Just as in the times of the New Testament, there will be people who are hurt and killed by abusive authorities, but God is still in control; if they were right with Him, and they will be ultimately rescued to the supreme security—home with God. . . . It is not an option to rebel against their authority. . . . God's people must be aware that they have a responsibility before God to respect, obey, and submit to His anointed servants. . . . Far too many with the church of Christ have imitated the words of Korah and other leaders of Israel who said to Moses, 'You have gone too far! The whole community is holy, everyone of them, and the Lord is with them. Why do you set yourself above the Lord's assembly?'. . . . It is true that all Christians walking in the light are holy and God is indeed with everyone of them. However, it is also true that through His spirit certain men have been assigned responsibilities to lead in the Kingdom and that to oppose them is to oppose God who anointed them.[1]

The Boston Movement teaches that each member should be answerable to another disciple in order to provide nurturing for new Christians. Members are encouraged to imitate and trust their disciplers.

A disciple is one who obeys his discipler even if he doesn't comprehend what he's told. Because he wants to have a teachable heart, he will fully obey and be totally obedient even if what he's asked to do is contrary to what he would normally do or think. To distrust the person God had put in his life is equal to distrusting God and his faith in God is shown by his faith in his discipler.[2]

In 1987, evangelist Kip McKean gave a talk entitled, "Why Do You Resist the Spirit?" in which he said, "No one can do it on their own. Everybody needs ongoing discipleship. You are a disciple of God until you die and you are a disciple of someone else until you die."[3]

The Boston Movement demands "Lordship baptism." In other words, one must confess Jesus as the Lord of every area of his life and demonstrate that he is a disciple before being baptized. This has resulted in a wave of rebaptisms, since new adherents who may have been baptized in another Christian church find that their previous baptism is not acceptable to the Boston Church of Christ. Even those people with backgrounds in the mainline Churches of Christ find themselves needing rebaptism.

The Boston Movement is an example of the elitist orientation that is so pervasive in authoritarian-church movements. It alone has the Truth, and to question its teachings and practices is to invite rebuke. As Jerry Jones observes:

> When the Boston Movement is confronted with their wrong teachings, its practice is to attack the character and life of the questioner by claiming that he has "sin in his life." Such terms as "prideful," "independent spirit," and "rebellious" are used in answer to the inquirer. The Boston Movement believes that being "independent" or "critical" is sin.[4]

Yeakley's research on the Boston Movement concluded that the disciple/discipler relationship was potentially manipulative and destructive. Because members are required to confess their sins to their disciplers, the emphasis on such self-disclosure can be dangerous.

> The discipling hierarchy thus becomes a glorified informant network. As such, it is an effective means of control. . . . Those being discipled were told what courses to take in school, what

field to major in, what career to enter, whom to date or not date, and even whom to marry or not marry.[5]

The spiritual elitism of abusive churches can be seen in some of the terminology they use to refer to themselves: "God's Green Berets," "God's End-Time Army," the "faithful remnant," the special "move of God." As one ex-member put it, "We believed we were on the cutting edge of what God was doing in the world. I looked down on people who left our movement; they didn't have what it took. They were not faithful to their commitment. When everyone else got with God's program, they would be involved in shepherding just like we were." A former member of a group known as The Assembly (headquartered in Fullerton, California, and discussed later in this book) said, "Although we didn't come right out and say it, in our innermost hearts we really felt that there was no place in the world like our assembly. We thought the rest of Christianity was out to lunch."

Community Chapel's Pastor Barnett regularly reminded his followers that their church was special. "We've got to go on into a new thing that God has promised in his Word that no church has ever come into yet. . . . Do you know of any other church in which people are loving each other with that same kind of unconditional love? I don't."

If abusive churches are exclusive and special, it follows that they will be targets for persecution, or so their leaders seem to feel. "It is the earmark of the last-day church that if God has promised it, and we are beginning to experience it, you know the devil's going to fight it."

Pastor Barnett would tell his flock: "You'll be a laughing stock, a mockery. You will find that there will be hatred toward you and it will come from the church world. You are sheep among wolves, and the wolves are the religious ones, the church world."

The leader of one controversial group named Aggressive Christianity Missions Training Corps complained, "The churches are full of sinners. We don't want to be hypocrites. You try to be strict and keep people clean, and everybody crucifies you. We're strict and we're not going to apologize for it. If we're crucified, we're crucified."

Jan was a member of a group that felt it was being unjustly persecuted by its critics, including the press. Here is her account of life with The Piecemakers, a small southern California communal-Christian group.

Jan had had all she was going to take. Eleven years of frustrated emotion, suppressed anger, and mental anguish came boiling out, and she began to swing her purse and bags of groceries at her tormentors—two "sisters" in the Body of Christ Fellowship, the informal name for The Piecemakers. They were "loving" her to repentance by screaming obscenities at her and attempting to "break through" to the point where she would again be submissive to the words and teachings of their unofficial leader, Marie Kolasinski. Although one of the women was nearly twice her size and holding her arms, Jan managed to break free, run to her room, and lock the door. Later, when her husband joined her, she said, "Mark, you have to get us and the kids out of here and away from these people."

The next morning Jan insisted that the six adults in her household meet to discuss who would be moving out. The two "sisters" wanted to postpone the meeting until the next day when Marie would be home from her family vacation in the mountains. Saying that she was "no fool," Jan stood her ground. The "sisters," as well as Jan's natural sister and brother-in-law who were also a part of the Fellowship, declared that they were staying and "claiming the land for God." Jan, as holder of the lease, knew otherwise.

That afternoon, twenty members of the Body of Christ Fellowship came to move the women out. In the process, they took everything that they believed had been bought with "God's money"—sheets off the beds, toilet paper holders out of the bathrooms, bolts and screws ripped right out of the walls. Jan's house was ransacked. Unfortunately, Mark was not home at the time.

Later, in the early evening, five of the "brothers" came back, saying they had come to claim "God's bed"—a youth bed on which Jan's youngest daughter slept. Not wanting them to trash the children's room, Jan asked if she could bring the bed downstairs. She was pushed out of the way by her brother, also a member of the Fellowship, and the men headed up the stairs. Grabbing her brother's arm and pleading with him, Jan was beaten to the floor. Another relative, who had come to stay and help Jan out, had her arm twisted behind her back until she cried, and was told to "Keep out of God's way!" Meanwhile, Jan's thirteen-year-old son, eldest of her six children, had run down to the kitchen, grabbed a butcher knife, and was on his way up the stairs to protect his mother. In the resulting chaos, the men left with the bed, and Jan and her children were left crying on the floor.

When Mark returned home, Jan asked the children not to tell him how roughly she had been treated, but the children told all. Mark responded by gathering his six children into his arms, saying, "It doesn't matter. We've only lost material things. I have what I've been praying for. My family is now free."

This dramatic account, tearfully related to me by Jan one month after her departure from the Body of Christ Fellowship, exemplifies the trauma of involvement in even the smallest of aberrational, abusive groups. The Body of Christ Fellowship, also known by their business name of Piecemakers Country Store, is located in Costa Mesa, California. Unofficially headed by grandmotherly Marie Kolasinski, who denies her leadership role ("God would strike me down if I took credit for his beautiful work"), the Body of Christ Fellowship is unique in its use of profanity, for Marie's edict that required vasectomies for male members, and for their claims that the second coming of Christ has "already come and gone."

Jan and her family were members of the Fellowship for eleven years. Most of her children were born during their involvement with the organization, which first began because Jan believed that members of the Fellowship had a "greater Christian walk." She felt that they were "walking in the fullness of life," and were growing closer to Jesus than was possible in other groups or churches. Her first encounter with Marie (she is known by no other title) came about through a mutual friend. Marie said, without ever having met her before, "Oh, Jan, take off your shoes for you are standing on holy ground."

In the early days, the group experienced healings, spoke in tongues, and conducted baptisms in a local swimming pool. However, somewhere along the line, Marie and the Fellowship began changing from a charismatic Bible study to a strict, authoritarian communal group. The change occurred gradually, with Marie slowly introducing teachings that contradicted the Bible.

While the group claims to live peacefully as a communal witness (they own several houses in the Costa Mesa area), their doctrine and practices have evolved over the years to a point of drastic departure from orthodoxy. Marie believes that she has "come through the veil"—that she experienced the death of her flesh in 1978 and now walks in sinless perfection. As the only one to have yet begun to "walk in the fullness," she dictates every aspect of the lives of her followers so that they too, some day, may join her in her exalted state. Consequently, she is beyond confrontation and in total control. "If you are sitting in this room today, and you are doubting whether or not these are the words of the Father, you better check to see if you are doing the will of God." She adds, "I always marvel at people who will come and hear the truth of what is going on in this fellowship and reject it."

As the only one yet to achieve sinless perfection, Marie is God's mouthpiece to her followers. Any questioning of her decisions or dissent is defined as the rebellion of the original sin nature in her followers and an indication of their lack of perfection. "Words" from God, received by Marie, are obeyed by her followers without question. Members have been known to surrender wedding rings, forsake their children, and move to different states, in obedience to Marie's received "words." Marie has also reportedly received "words" telling members to give money to her husband for his failing business, or to refrain from styling another's hair after she received a poor haircut.

According to Marie's philosophy, growing closer to God requires suffering. This means the travail and pain of letting go of everything of one's old life—family relationships, both immediate and extended; personal belongings of sentimental value; and the ability to control one's life and make personal decisions. The more broken her members, the closer they are to "entering into God." Therefore, every aspect of their personal lives and egos is systematically assaulted.

One of Marie's assistants indicated that members cry and go through so much emotional and spiritual torture because it is a painful process to shed all of life's pleasures in order to serve God. Jackie Kindschi, Marie's childhood friend and former member of the Fellowship, was quoted in a local newspaper as saying:

> Marie believes, and so do the others, that when they pick on a person and break them down, they are helping them get closer to God. She really thinks she is doing the right thing. . . . When I look around my apartment and see all the things I "idolize," like my children and grandchildren, my memories and my material items, all the things that Marie says we shouldn't have, I say hallelujah.[6]

Marie's brother and sister-in-law are also very concerned. "Somewhere along the line Marie got messed up with drugs, and the next time we saw her, she was the leader of this group." They did attend some of the meetings at the fellowship but decided the group was not for them. "Everything is contrary to scriptural teachings and she twists them to fit her cause. She is holding those people hostage and threatens them with God."[7]

Marie now believes and claims that she "holds the keys to the Kingdom," and has the power to regulate who and who will not have the opportunity to go to heaven. Jan says that her manipulation is "total and complete," and that there is no possibility of members winning against her. In the "fullness" there is neither right nor wrong, good nor bad; therefore, anything that Marie does or says is perfect.

Since "dying to the flesh" allows Jesus Christ to be born in a person in fullness (the supposed second coming of Christ according to Marie), those individuals who have come or are coming "through the veil" should no longer live "fleshly" lives. Therefore, members of the Body of Christ abstain from sexual relationships with their spouses since there is neither male nor female nor marriage in the Kingdom of God.

"Natural man must shed all his ways to reach God. The flesh must die in order for us to gain entry into the Kingdom of God. I'm celibate and am no longer a slave to any man, lust, or desire. Only God is in my thoughts now."[8]

Conceiving and bearing children are both considered to be sorrowful ordeals. Marie believes that humankind evolved from the animals, so that having children is "reproducing after one's lustful flesh." Children therefore keep one from seeking God; one needs rather to have "spiritual children." Needless to say, the children in the Body of Christ Fellowship do not lead normal lives, usually being separated from their parents. Marie states that God himself is "trying to tear down the family unit."

Living out their commitment to God, members rise each day at 5:15 A.M. They meet at 5:30 A.M. to walk for two miles, then receive the day's instructions from Marie at her home. Members are assigned to either work at Piecemakers, do manual labor through the Village Tilers, a home improvement arm of Piecemakers, or baby-sit a host of children. Members' weekly salary is ten dollars and no free time is allowed. Jan says that, "Every minute of the day was accounted for. If you were supposed to be somewhere, you were there and no one argued."

Portions of the day are spent in meetings to learn about God and scold errant members. These "scoldings" can last for hours and include being labeled a "slut" or a "whore," if one is a woman, or being convinced that one is weak and worthless, if one is a man. Accompanying the scoldings are outpourings of profanity, the use of which, one therapist believes, breaks down religious training so that victims are more open to Marie's influence.

Those who supposedly attempt to usurp Marie's authority are the most severely abused by brutal group-humiliation tactics and peer pressure. "They would hit you blindside, and you never knew it was coming. All the members would gather around and begin screaming and hollering obscenities until you broke," says one former member.[9] There are also allegations of physical beatings. However, Marie claims that only by their strength and adherence to the word of God, and submission to her authority, will members overcome and be successful. Success is defined as the return of all that one has given up to "go through the veil."

Interestingly, Marie's husband, Ray, is Catholic and not a member of the Body of Christ Fellowship. Jan states that while Marie preaches against family, she is a submissive wife to Ray, cooking his dinner, keeping his house, and attending Mass at his side. However, Jan also notes that at the point Marie received the word about communal living and the pooling of resources, Ray needed money to pay his taxes. The pooled funds allegedly went to pay Ray's tax debt, among other things.

The straw that finally broke the camel's back for Jan was watching her own sister and another woman verbally abuse and attack her mother with gross profanity. Why? Because she wanted to bring Christmas presents to her grandchildren. Jan thought, "This can't be what religion and Jesus are all about. This isn't what he died on the cross for." Her altercation with the other persons of her household came shortly thereafter. Within a few days, she and her family had escaped.

Marie claims that Jan is bitter because she was not strong enough to "walk with God." She told Jan that she would "turn into a whore, an alcoholic, and a drug addict," that she would be "crazy within six weeks, just like your mother," and that her husband would be "chasing everything in a skirt."[10]

Jan and her family had to move out of the area to escape constant threats and harassment from members and Marie. Although they have been away from Marie Kolasinski and the Body of Christ Fellowship for over six years, the emotional scars and spiritual turmoil are only now fading away. There is still guilt over influencing four of her siblings to become involved in the group. She has only recently regained her "vision for God." And she and her family have only just recently returned to church. But they are free.

7

LIFE-STYLE AND
EXPERIENCE
ABUSIVE CHURCHES
FOSTER RIGIDITY

7

LIFE-STYLE AND
EXPERIENCE
Abusive Churches
Foster Rigidity

Tom and Pam Murray are still searching for God and the truth after their seven-year experience with what has been called the No-Name Fellowship, or C-U (Champaign-Urbana) Ministries, titles that originated with the media for a group of Christian believers who considered themselves to be just a "part of the body of Christ and therefore did not believe a name for [our] group was necessary." Tom says that even after two years out of the group he is still working through a lot of experiences in his mind, "trying to discern what was good and what was bad; attempting to save and retain that which was profitable and releasing that which was unprofitable." Of one thing he is sure, sincerity does not guarantee that God will always honor your actions.

What began as a Bible study, organized by a few students who felt the established churches were weak and ineffectual examples of Christianity, evolved into a rigidly structured group with one man giving basically all the direction. As is typical of some authoritarian groups, the No-Name Fellowship consisted of white, middle- to upper-middle-class young people from eighteen to twenty-five years of age, of above-average intelligence, well educated, and highly idealistic.

Doug Kleber was chief elder in all but name. It was generally recognized that he had experienced a "greater calling of God" than had the other elders and, consequently, much of what the members practiced in the daily routine of their lives stemmed directly from "revelation" that Doug received, or from additional "revelation" that was received by others on the subjects on which he had broken ground. These extra-biblical "revelations" dictated how members were to properly eat, dress, discipline their children, decorate their homes, clean their homes, and behave in the marriage bed. Because of the group members' love of the Lord and their genuine seeking to know and do what he wanted, they submitted to Kleber's self-appointed spiritual authority, even though at times Pam knew that he was wrong. As time went on, she eventually convinced herself that she "was the one that was always wrong."

It was generally recognized that Kleber had always had a dominating presence about him, even from youth. It was said that at one time a number of prophetic words had been spoken over him indicating that God had called him to lead people. Tom never believed, nor does he now believe, that there was any "deliberate" motive to coerce or control people on Kleber's part. "I still believe that this man's heart was free from any deliberate intention to lead us in any way for his own personal gain, financially or psychologically."

Pam, however, knew that something was "off," but she couldn't label what was wrong. "I appreciated receiving direction, being a new wife and mother. I felt so loved by the brethren. We were all in it together. I don't believe that *all* the fault for the group lies in the leader's lap."

Consistent with a number of similar groups, Pam and Tom's fellowship attempted to live according to "first-century-church" standards. They believed that "the stain of the world" was upon the established church. "Many of us who were zealous for God found it easy to separate ourselves from other churches, other Christians, families, and friends because of what we saw happening in the mainline churches."

In a very revealing statement, Pam and Tom observe: "If there didn't exist a real lack in the organized church today, you probably wouldn't have the 'backlash' effect involving thousands of well-meaning young Christians." This "backlash" resulted in members of the No-Name Fellowship believing that they were the only devoted and pure body of

believers around. They became distrustful and contemptu-
ous of almost everyone, and believed that most people were
wicked or misguided hypocrites destined for eternal damnation. "We became victims of zealousness without knowledge." Tom now takes a more balanced approach to the
biblical notion of separation from the world. "There is a
place for elitism in the church if it's wrapped in wisdom and
understanding."

As Pam looks back on the experience, she finds it hard to
believe that when people called her brainwashed, she took it
as a compliment. "We were blessed to have a clean mind.
But it did reach a point where I didn't decide things on my
own. Even vacations had to be cleared with the leadership.
You wouldn't dare leave without God's blessing. And the
elders would be called to okay the house we wanted to rent."
She now understands that "trying to make thirty-five house-
wives clean, decorate and dress the same way didn't leave
room for expressions of individuality" that are a normal part
of the diversity of the Christian church. She also understands
that the enforced cutting of almost all ties with family and
friends outside of the fellowship was not God's way of
"separating oneself from the stain of the world."

As parents and others began to react to the isolationist
stance that the fellowship was taking, members began to
believe that the "world was out to get them." "Parents
kidnapped their kids to have them deprogrammed, which in
turn stirred up the media and local authorities with the end
result being that all these circumstances only solidified our
intitial convictions. No one thought that this was anything
but the normal sequence of events that an end-time church
was supposed to go through." As far as those on the inside
were concerned, the critics "just didn't understand." Members felt that "no one could ever get the full story unless they
came in person to find out for themselves how we lived." Of
course, no one was ever given the opportunity to see the real
group dynamics.

Over the course of time, as Kleber received more and more
"revelations," life became increasingly rigid and difficult.
The control mechanisms employed by the leadership covered a broad spectrum of behavior including dress, diet,

work habits, personal style or mannerisms, prayer, Bible study, fasting, entertainment, jobs, and whether or not to have children. "There wasn't one area in our lives where we weren't legalistic about something." Tom reflects, "It seems strange that during our time in the fellowship, you would think that the overwhelming evidence in the New Testament concerning grace would have had some effect upon our minds concerning these rigidities." However, there was so much "revelation" coming that the average member found it impossible to take the time necessary to carefully study the Bible to determine for him or herself that what was being taught was the whole truth of God. In addition, as Pam notes, "I lived in fear of correction, while Scripture tells us to embrace and love it." Also, many of the rules and regulations were never actually spoken or articulated as a command. One simply knew from experience that something was a rule, and, if not adhered to, discipline resulted.

Given the overwhelming amount of "revelation" that Kleber supposedly received, "the tendency was to trust first and then hope that you could find the time to search the Word in prayer and verify or refute whatever particular issue was being discussed." The term "revelation teaching" as used in the group did not signify a special, dramatic, prophetic utterance, but had to do with accumulated spiritual knowledge and insight from the Bible that the leadership claimed to receive from the Holy Spirit, some of which was merely the pastor's attempt to relate Scripture to everyday life. For these folk, the meaning of Scripture is not simply that which the intellect understands from reading, but is apprehended ultimately by revelation from the Holy Spirit. For example, when it was announced that women should not wear jeans, it came not as an isolated pronouncement, but was based on a continuing series of "revelational teachings" that, layer upon layer, gradually readied the congregation for directives that might seem strange to outsiders.

Life became increasingly based on experience and not on the standards of Scripture. Conscience became externalized and embodied in Kleber and the other elders. At the same time members were taught not to trust their feelings, intuition, and emotions, lest they find themselves "walking in the flesh." "We stifled the voice of God within, mistaking common-sense reactions for the 'rising up of the flesh.'" Tom believes that "It was probably this very doctrine that disabled most of us from ever obeying the 'gut feelings' of apprehension within. Many times we stifled our own conscience in the desire to walk spiritually." For Pam, who had had an active prayer life before the fellowship, "God turned into an unreachable spirit. It was like playing a game that I could never win." She has lost all desire to share Jesus with others.

If members ever did decide they had reason to disagree with Kleber and his "revelations," they quickly found reason to stop. Pam knew that even when she desired to stand and say, "This is crazy!" or, "I don't agree!" she would have been disciplined for disrupting and coming against authority.

Women of C-U Ministries were totally submissive to males and were barred from leadership or decision-making roles, as well as from work outside the home. Pam says that, "It got to the point where what I had to say usually got suppressed because I knew it was a waste of time to discuss it. I'd lose." Tom, no doubt reflecting his status as a male in the group, takes a more moderate view on how dissent was handled. "There never seemed to be a great deal of major dissent on most issues, and when dissent did appear, it wasn't of the type that endangered the fabric of the fellowship. In fact, it occurred rather often in the course of meetings and was generally settled by the breaking of the Word."

Although the "breaking of the Word" may have been a part of the settling of dissenting opinion, outrageous discipline of members was the order of the day according to Pam and other ex-members. These measures included the spanking of adults with hands, belts, wooden paddles, or other objects; the drinking of salt water; having liquid soap squirted into a woman's mouth for inappropriately addressing her husband; and lying at someone's feet in order to apologize. Pam recalls a women's prayer meeting at which one woman was told to remove her dress in order to become "more vulnerable."

Fear, guilt, and intimidation all played a role in the disciplinary process. Obedience to the standard of the group

was secured by the fear of divine judgment. For the most
part, the internalized psychological and spiritual discipline
applied by the group was enough to bring about the desired
results. But on quite a number of occasions, verbal public
humiliation and sometimes physical public humiliation were
used to help straighten out deviant behavior. Tom adds,
"Many, but not all, of these disciplinary measures took place
in front of the entire body, because we regarded ourselves a
family. Many times the body was asked to judge whether
they thought the offender had found repentance."

Unfortunately, the harshness of the discipline extended to
the children as well. Pam says, "I could cry over some of the
spankings they received. Bruised bottoms. They were even
calloused." The eventual disbanding of the church was in
large part related to a tragic event that took place in another
branch of the organization in Spokane, Washington. (At one
point the group also had outposts in Passaic, New Jersey, and
Plano, Texas.)

In December of 1987, ten-year-old Aaron Norman died as
a result of medical neglect and a beating administered by his
father and Doug Kleber. The boy suffered from juvenile
diabetes but his parents did not obtain medical care for him,
preferring to rely on the healing power of prayer. When his
physical condition worsened and prayer did not seem to be
effective, elders of the church were consulted to determine
what the problem was. According to a story in the June 21,
1988 issue of the *Chicago Tribune*, the elders determined
that Aaron had sinned. The sin was masturbation, but Aaron
would not confess to the sin. His father decided to spank
Aaron with a board because the Holy Spirit had told him that
he had been masturbating. As the Spokane County deputy
prosecutor stated, "His father and the elders 'rebuked' Aaron
to confess, but he wouldn't. Aaron's father and Kleber then
beat the child. . . . A wooden paddle was used at some point
until Aaron confessed. On Sunday morning when his parents
awoke, Aaron was dead. There were severe bruises on his
buttocks."

The Murrays left the fellowship when it "all blew up in
our faces." If the fellowship hadn't broken up, they feel they
would probably still be there. "We really didn't have a clue

that anything was wrong." They have had a difficult time since leaving because they had been programmed to believe that to exit the group was to leave family. Members who had left previously were said to be "deceived and going to hell." The faithful who remained prayed that the defectors would suffer calamities to prove to them that they had been wrong. According to Pam, "Since we believed so strongly that the group was 'The One,' contemplating leaving wasn't even in your thoughts. Rather, we had a fear of doing something wrong and being *told* to leave!"

Pam went through a time after leaving when she wondered if God even existed. They both have had difficulty in returning to church. Tom admits, "I'm not sure if I'll ever understand why God allowed it to happen, but his grace and mercy are sufficient enough to satisfy us when there aren't any answers to the questions that we still ask."

Tom Murray gives a final warning: "It is foolish to think that you can remain objective in an abusive-church situation for any length of time without being subtly influenced. No one can consider themselves above the possibility of deception."

There is another "nameless" group, much larger than the one just discussed, which also engages in various forms of spiritual and physical abuse. Very little has been written about this obscure worldwide church which is said to have as many as one hundred thousand members. It was founded at the turn of the century by a Scottish coal miner named William Irvine who was later joined by Edward Cooney, an Irishman. In the early days, the group was referred to as the "Cooneyites," and later became known both as the "Two-by-Two's" (because its itinerant preachers or "workers" travel in pairs) and the "Nameless House Sect." The group deplores denominationalism and "man-made" doctrines. It identifies with no name and claims only to follow Jesus Christ.[1]

Former members, who often refer to it as "the Truth," claim that a great number of children raised in the movement are subjected to stern discipline from an early age in order that their "wills can be broken." Ex-members report that infants as young as three months old are swatted. One said that

> fussing of small children is an unacceptable disruption of the meeting, so children must be taught quickly and firmly how to behave and be silent. Children are expected to behave as miniature adults and whatever must be done to achieve this end is done. One common discipline is to expect children to eat everything on their plates, to train them for the task of being in the "work." Forcing children to eat is considered part of breaking their wills and teaching them to submit to parental authority. If they refuse or cannot, the workers view it as rebellion.[2]

Like many other abusive churches, the Two-by-Two's impose a restrictive and rigorous life-style on the membership. Women adherents shun makeup and wear long, uncut hair wrapped tightly in buns on the tops of their heads. Jewelry is proscribed, while plain dresses are the norm. Slacks, shorts, and sleeveless blouses are forbidden in public. They submit to the men of the group who tend to wear dark-colored clothes and carry black-covered King James Versions of the Bible. Marriages are performed by civil authorities only, since church "workers" do not register with state officials.[3]

Conformity to a strict life-style is expected of all children and young people in the Truth. They are discouraged from participating in after-school sports and other social activities. Their circle of friends does not extend beyond the group.

> They often grow up ignorant and unaware of current affairs around them. One woman remembers taking her young son to the doctor who was astonished that the boy knew nothing about Big Bird or other Sesame Street characters. Another woman relates that her son's kindergarten teacher was shocked that he hadn't ever heard of Easter. . .[most Two-by-Two's do not observe Christmas or Easter]. This lack of awareness, culturally, religiously, politically, and socially, severely stunts their perceptions of the world around them. . . . Emotional withdrawal and social isolation are

typical responses among children in the Truth which are carried forward into adulthood.[4]

———————————◦•◆•◦———————————

Members of the University Bible Fellowship were encouraged to get rid of their stereos. One student threw his six-hundred-dollar stereo receiver into Lake Michigan and exclaimed, "I felt so free after that." An ex-member of another abusive church tells of being advised to get rid of her dead husband's spirit by burning her wedding pictures, selling her wedding ring, and giving away their bed. "Our children watched their baby dolls and stuffed animals get fried in a bonfire," reports one ex-member, whose former church taught that such attachments could become "idols" and therefore represented potential sin.

Life-style rigidity in abusive churches often manifests itself in a curiously reactive mode with regard to sexuality. Proscriptive measures reveal a sometimes bizarre preoccupation with sex that mental-health professionals would no doubt conclude gives evidence of repression. For example, an ex-member of Faith Tabernacle, a now defunct California church pastored by Eleanor Daries,[5] was told she had to give up playing the cello because of the "sexual positioning" required to play the intrument. Members of the University Bible Fellowship (UBF) were urged to repent of their sinful desires and cut off their relationships with boyfriends and girlfriends. Those who dated were called "wolfy men" or "foxy women" and were considered to be full of "flesh desires." Another authoritarian group provides written guidelines for male/female behavior in church: "Limit physical contact in church to hand-holding. Snuggling, cuddling, laying the head on his shoulder, if longer than a second or so, is not appropriate. Excessive massaging of one another is not appropriate."

The women of Community Chapel, in printed instructions dated September 1978 and titled, "Perspectives on Dress Conduct," were given detailed guidelines about underwear, fingernails, and make-up. Under the heading, "Breasts," we read: "No exposure of cleavage showing. Examine what is exposed when bending over; nothing should be seen. Consider also exposure when sitting and swinging around. Small-chested gals need to be extra careful." Under the entry on fingernails: "Color should be subtle and natural, not deep, bright, or unusual colors." Women of Community Chapel were instructed to "let the Pastor take the initiative to hug, but feel free to hug him if there is a great, proper need." In view of what transpired in that particular church a few years later, these kinds of "guidelines" appear now to be rather tame.

In that same church, Community Chapel, the pastor at one point included these specific regulations in the Sunday bulletin: "Remember our rule: All women who show up at the church offices should be dressed femininely, and if they are wearing slacks, those slacks should be definitely feminine, complemented by feminine tops and feminine shoes. . . . Please respect the right of your shepherd to guide you into more appropriate, conservative, and feminine dress." Men of the church were not overlooked. The church bookstore sold a pamphlet entitled, "Jesus Had Short Hair!" The bulletin advised males to "avoid low cut and unbuttoned shirts, jeans, beards, unkempt hair, long fancy sideburns, and frizzy hair." Neither sex could wear amulets or crosses.

While mainstream evangelical churches have always encouraged a life of holiness before the Lord and urged moderation in dress and other aspects of life-style, authoritarian churches demonstrate an excessive focus on such concerns. The restricted life-style and limits on personal freedom that follow are just other examples of the need to control that all abusive churches exemplify. Conformity to prescribed standards is achieved, more so than in mainline churches, through peer pressure and pastoral directives.

As we have already seen, some of these pastoral directives and announcements border on the ridiculous, and to the outsider they are both puzzling and amusing. For example, Hobart Freeman, former pastor of Faith Assembly (not affiliated with the Assemblies of God), told his flock that wearing striped running shoes was considered to be homosexual fashion. He also announced that members should not use the terminology "pregnant woman." According to Freeman, only cows become pregnant; women are "with child." The Sunday bulletin of one California church contained the following announcement: "Mrs. Blank [I have changed her real name] refuses to stop the soul-damning sin of gluttony. She uses every excuse to stay fat. She also has a bitter, complaining attitude toward this church. The Board of Elders recommends that she be transferred to [another church] until she is willing to stop her sin of gluttony. The members of this church will vote on dropping and barring Mrs. Blank next Sunday. . . . If Mrs. Blank wishes to repent, she needs to see [the leadership] and express a willingness to stop complaining and lose weight."

In my research of abusive churches, I never cease to be amazed at the degree to which private and personal concerns are made public and brought to the attention of the congregation. In a relatively small organization known as "Rejoyce [sic] in Jesus Ministries," the members were asked to pray for two named individuals "and their finances." Then the bulletin proceeded to announce: "This past week, checks that they wrote out to RJM bounced. Note: If you have written a check to RJM that has bounced, please get in touch with the RJM Office regarding repaying the original amount plus charges resulting from your bounced check."

Seattle's Community Chapel distributed a bulletin insert entitled, "Guidelines for Dancing Before the Lord." It contained detailed instructions for adults and children pertaining to the expected conduct of members while participating in dancing during the worship services. "Do not obstruct aisles or block vision; return immediately to your seat after dancing. Keep 'locked into' Jesus during worship, but be watchful for collisions. If it is crowded, confine your movements to a smaller area. . . . Watch where you swing your arms."

The guidelines also provide for those who are not physically fit. "If you are new to the athletic moves of dancing in the Spirit, be careful of overdoing it at first. Stretch tight muscles before and after use. Some people find that elastic ankle and knee braces help if these areas are weak or sore." The policy statement also notes that, "Because of the limited

space and the number of those wanting to dance during the
service, the pastor wants the most gifted to be in the front
area during service, and not more at once than the area can
accommodate without the dancers having to fear collisions."
And finally, "Ushers and elders should be notified when
people violate our rules. We do not want to allow misconduct
to continue or proliferate."

A final example of legalism within authoritarian churches
can be seen in the list of regulations that one particular
network of churches imposes on those who attend "training"
sessions. I have selected just a few from a lengthy list to give
you a sense of the control exercised by this group:

- No unexcused absences from any of the meetings will be
  tolerated.
- All the trainees must be seated in the meetings in strict
  accordance with their assigned seat number.
- All the trainees must be in their seats at least five minutes
  before the start of each meeting.
- No eating, drinking, or gum chewing will be tolerated
  after the start of the meeting.
- No trainee is allowed to leave his seat for any reason
  (including rest room) during the course of a meeting,
  except for emergency.
- All the trainees are charged to participate in no gossip or
  negative talk against any individual or any church.
- All the trainees must rest each afternoon and not go out to
  visit, shop, etc.

Although most authoritarian churches adhere to a strict
regimen of do's and don'ts, there are a few exceptions. I have
talked to a number of former members of the Christian
Growth Ministries shepherding movement who have indicated that quite a bit of flexibility was applied to the area of
drinking behavior. In fact, in some shepherding circles,
drinking was almost promoted and drunkenness trivialized.
One ex-member of a church affiliated with Charles Simpson,
who at the time was still with Christian Growth Ministries,
describes it this way: "In the early 1980s, a bunch of us
began to go out drinking for some innocent fun. Even
drunkenness was not looked upon as a bad thing. One of our
sayings was, 'It's not what you do, it's who you do it with.'"

If life-style rigidity is a characteristic of most abusive churches, the role of subjective experience is equally crucial in understanding how such groups drift toward religious marginality. In the second chapter we discussed the pervasive influence of spiritual experience in the life of Community Chapel. Earlier in this chapter we noted how the lives of Tom and Pam Murray were impacted not only by outrageous discipline, but also by "revelation teaching," and the primacy of experience. Another group that recently dissolved as an international federation of churches, but which illustrates the importance of subjective experience, is Maranatha Christian Ministries. Here is the account of one young woman's spiritual quest in that organization.

———————•◆••———————

Karen Moore left Maranatha Christian Ministries (MCM) after three years of dedicated service to what she believed was God's work. Having moved up in the ranks of leadership, she was responsible for the lives of fourteen other young women as their "discipler," or "shepherdess." She could no longer reconcile the dichotomy between the God she once knew and the one she served with fear in MCM.

Karen joined MCM after two years of experiencing depression and a sense of purposelessness that came on the heels of several life changes. She had graduated from nursing school, ended a seven-year relationship, and began to lose her network of friends after the disbanding of her campus fellowship. She was at an extremely vulnerable stage in her life, in need of some stability that her new-found Maranatha friends seemed to provide. Through MCM she found loving people, a Christian value system, goals and direction, leadership, and tremendous support. In exchange, she gave up her will, her ability to think critically, and her relationships with family and former friends.

Karen came to MCM with numerous doubts and reservations concerning the teachings in the group, although she was impressed by its radical nature. She believed in being totally committed to God, but was concerned about what she perceived as an excessive emphasis on holiness, faith, victory, "overcoming," and a lack of balance with regard to mercy, grace, and love. She initially believed that she could provide this balance for the group.

Her early skepticism was labeled as "mind idolatry" accompanied, the leadership told her, by spirits of critical thinking, independence, rebellion, and mistrust. These so-called "spirits" were exorcised from her at the beginning of her time with MCM, and any further objections to MCM doctrine or practice were merely recurring manifestations of those very same spirits. Thus, Karen's abilities to think critically and evaluate were effectively stifled.

As she was further indoctrinated into God's "higher plan," she learned that her mind had been totally perverted by the Fall and that it was completely unreliable. Depression, she was told, was a sign of spiritual oppression. Anger was sin, unless it was directed at outsiders, in which case it was probably righteous. Above all, she came to understand that submission to MCM leadership was essential.

Each member of MCM was under the direction of a "discipler" or "shepherd" who, in turn, was under the authority of other leaders in a pyramidal, hierarchical struc-ture. Robert Weiner, MCM's founder, was at its head. Every aspect of life was to be under total submission to the leadership, whether having to do with family visits, "accept-able" literature, marriage, and even female hygiene. Disobe-dience to the leaders was seen as rebellion, which was equated with the sin of witchcraft.

As time went on, Karen discovered that whereas she once loved God with open affection and awe, now she was scared and intimidated by him. As she moved up in leadership, she found herself explaining the teachings of MCM to new members so that they sounded less harsh, reassuring them that abiding by the teachings was really pleasant and fulfilling. At the same time, she realized that while she once was able to discern God's will personally, she now was told that her leaders knew God's will for her better than she knew it herself. Unfortunately, their answers supposedly representing God's will were often contrary to those she knew deep down to be biblical. Examples of such "answers" were that "reading books by non-Christians would reap corruption"; that she had "to get permission to visit my grandmother, or to travel at all. If I wanted to visit relatives out of town, I was to submit that to my shepherdess who would take it to the pastor for confirmation. If he agreed it was from God for me to visit, I was then permitted to do so"; that "I was no longer to be alone on my days off or anytime" [because the devil was trying to attack her]; and, that "I could more easily be deceived because I was a woman."

Friendships outside of MCM were terminated, except within the framework of evangelism. One was permitted to develop friendships only for the purpose of witnessing. To "draw life from" loving relationships outside the group was felt to contradict the command to keep oneself unstained by the world. Other Christians could conceivably fellowship with members of MCM, but it was believed that they had such a lower revelation of God that it was repeatedly asked, "How can two walk together who do not share the same vision?"

In time, Karen felt that love became wholly conditioned upon her behavior. She was no longer heard unless she was presenting the party line, all else being considered evil and severely confronted as rebellion against the leadership and ultimately against God. The MCM vision became god, and everything was to be sacrificed to it. "The work" was important, but individuals were not. Members were expected to dress like overcomers, smile like overcomers, serve like overcomers, and behave like overcomers. Outsiders, particularly Christians who did not know them well, marveled at members' faith, victory, generosity, and obedience. Maranatha members had a high view of their own organization, considering themselves "God's Green Berets."

Upon making her decision to leave, Karen was overcome with thoughts of guilt and doubt as she agonized over conflicting feelings. To leave was to break covenant with MCM—an unforgiveable sin. To leave was to jeopardize the movement of God in MCM, and to endanger her salvation as well as the salvation of her outside friends and family. An overreaction to problems within the group could be costly. Was she lost in carnal, soulish, selfish pride? And, as a woman, was she as easily deceived as her MCM brothers had said? Her fourteen disciples might backslide. She also knew that her character would be defamed by the leadership if she left. They would announce that she was a false teacher, a false prophetess, one who never knew the Lord, just like others who had left before her. Her publicly confessed "sins" would be brought up as evidence against her. Perhaps Satan had come against her with great force to keep her from her ministry. Maybe a strong spirit of deception had come to blind her to God's mighty call upon her life, to distract her from her obviously close relationship with him.

As these doubts filled her mind, her pastors fed her additional guilt and psychological intimidation. Regardless of the doubting, after many days of fasting and prayer Karen could not honestly say that God had shown her any sin of which to repent, contrary to the counsel of her pastors. She had not read any non-Christian books, nor was there anything which she was not willing to give up for God that had become an idol. Yet she had been told that she had let Satan have an open door to her heart, and that she must repent and renounce him so that she could get on with God's will and continue as a full-time worker in the ministry.

Karen's decision to leave, as told to her small group of disciples, was quickly communicated to her pastor, Mark. Initial attempts to sway her with kindness and encouragement soon gave way to accusations of lack of trust for the leaders God had given her. There were dark predictions of her future, veiled threats, and eventual disfellowshipping. There was no place for her in MCM unless she repented— and submitted. Eternal damnation hinged on her decision.

Karen fully expected her plane to crash as she flew home to her parents. The wrath of God, according to her pastors in MCM, was upon her. Gone were the smiles, the assurances, the optimism for an alternate life-style that was far superior to ordinary life. Gone were the prophesies about being part of God's end-time army, and the supposed opportunities to reign with Jesus in the Holy of Holies reserved for His called-out ones. The young people in MCM were to be "the future great Christian leaders, full of power and grace and truth, that would lead the other unenlightened Christians through the coming Tribulation." Karen was told that all she now wanted was "to be married and to be a rich, mediocre suburbanite." Feeling that she could not continue in the group and maintain her relationship with God, Karen was forced to choose between serving him and "breaking covenant" with "his people." On January 18, 1981, Karen Moore walked away from "the Vision" of Maranatha Christian Ministries.

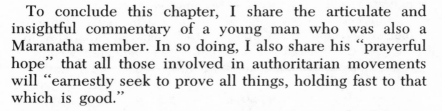

To conclude this chapter, I share the articulate and insightful commentary of a young man who was also a Maranatha member. In so doing, I also share his "prayerful hope" that all those involved in authoritarian movements will "earnestly seek to prove all things, holding fast to that which is good."

The most significant problems with Maranatha stem directly from its interwoven concepts of discipleship and submission to authority, which, I feel, have resulted in serious, destructive abuse.

In Maranatha the centrality of authority is a natural consequence of a military self-perception. Greater emphasis is placed upon building the "army of God" than nurturing and developing the "family of God." The leadership sees itself as setting up a new order on earth in the prospect of bringing in the kingdom of God, thereby establishing an external purified order in this age.

Preparation of leaders is obtained as quickly as is physically possible under the guise of ministry or spiritual expertise culminating in a sink-or-swim survival of the fittest environment. The often painful results in Maranatha include a lack of leaders with a mature understanding of the Bible. Because of this, unwarranted authority is attached to the contemporary spoken word, the *rhema*, going so far as to hold that it is equal to the written Word, the *logos*.

All too often the public revelation in the Bible is subordinated by the private revelations of the leadership of Maranatha, pointing not beyond themselves to Christ crucified and risen, but to the leadership's own experience. Unfortunately, this can lead to setting goals to possess the life of God in exclusively ecstatic experience.

On the emotional or mental level, the Maranatha environment encourages spiritually and experientially oriented persons to allow phenomena to determine their faith instead of interpreting experience with reason in light of Scripture. The "swallow-follow" concept, the "mind idolatry' teaching, and the overall dictatorial exercise of authority all combine to form a totalitarian attitude that behavior is determined solely by unfettered and thoughtless obedience and submission to authority. When the mind and the values of knowledge and understanding are rejected, downplayed, and scorned as being "rebellious," the mind becomes subverted and the will is subdued into passivity, producing a dangerous phenomenon many refer to as "mind control." The potential and, in fact, recurrent result is a mass production of stymied personalities. Consideration and appraisal of the individual by authority is effected through the capricious, demanding, and judgmental eyes of condemnation rather than the eyes of compassion, understanding, and mercy. Motivation becomes fear-oriented, not love-oriented.

Faith is transformed from an adventure into a duty as concern for righteousness through holiness and blind adherence to proscribed behavioral codes begin to envelop the individual's identity. Holy living becomes a pretext for a new legalism; keeping "the law" tends to become an end in itself rather than a means of service to God.

8

DISSENT AND DISCIPLINE
ABUSIVE CHURCHES
DISCOURAGE QUESTIONS

8

DISSENT AND DISCIPLINE
Abusive Churches
Discourage Questions

"I'll never forget, as long as I live, that feeling the first morning when I woke up there at the [River of Life] ranch and stared at that ceiling. I said, 'Oh God! I've really done this.' And, after a couple of days, I remember thinking to myself, 'Boy, I've really blown it.' But it was kind of like, 'Well, here we go, I'm just gonna trust God.'"

This was only the beginning of Paul and MaryAnn Hasting's negative experiences with Ed Mitchell's River of Life Ministries. Months of preparation had gone into their being influenced to "lay down everything they had to walk with Jesus." They were wooed and courted by Mitchell and his indoctrinated followers with public-relations techniques that would rival those of Madison Avenue. Eventually, their succumbing cost them everything, including their home, retirement monies, jobs, lost wages, and very nearly their family. They also exited River of Life almost eight thousand dollars in debt—and with River of Life creditors after them for organizational purchases.

Paul, an educator of thirteen years experience with a master's degree in educational psychology and a professional credential in pupil-personnel counseling, had limited Christian experience before his involvement with River of Life. He and his wife MaryAnn had been brought up Catholic, but they were not devout adherents. Their involvement began when River of Life was called The Centurion Door, and was based in Thousand Oaks, California. Attendance at that point was some three hundred persons. MaryAnn was the head of a liturgical-dance troupe called Hallelujah Dancers, and was having some personal difficulties when she heard of The Centurion Door as being a place to go for "counseling." As her involvement increased, the Hastings opened their home to prayer meetings. It was at that point that Ed Mitchell became involved in their lives and began inviting them to River of Life's ten-acre Apple Valley Ranch.

Mitchell, "tall, good looking, and charismatic," was developing an "end-times ministry" at the ranch, a place where people could come when society fell apart. There, Paul, MaryAnn, and their family found the people to be very loving and accepting. "We played volleyball, had barbecues, and had tremendous religious experiences. Over the period of the next couple of months, we would go out there on weekends. It was wonderful. It was something I had never experienced in my life before."

Over the months, as the Hastings' longings for significance, friendship, and "a return to Eden" were seemingly fulfilled, there were also subtle messages given concerning their commitment to Christ. There was the constant pressure to join "the group that had laid down everything they had to walk for Jesus Christ." Eventually they concluded, "What could be greater than to give one's life to Jesus Christ and the spread of the Gospel." Paul turned in his letter of resignation to the school district; they began the process of selling their home. Then the real pressures started.

Paul's resignation was extremely difficult for him. He had been told by Ed Mitchell that when he quit he would experience great emotional turmoil, but that he should realize this was Satan's ploy to keep him from accepting "God's call." Having internalized the group's initial indoctrination, Paul spiritualized his anxieties as the devil's attacks and then interpreted chance readings of scriptural passages as messages from God to go to the ranch. He was anointed as "pastor of the ranch" by Mitchell, who then began speaking of himself as "the major end-time Apostle."

Paul was also going to be the principal of the ranch's new school, and also the counselor to the many seekers who came to the facility. However, as Paul states, "Everything inside of me was just screaming out against it. Everything. I woke up that night. . .and I lay there for three hours rebuking Satan. I felt sick to my stomach. And then I had what I felt were some visions that were pointing me to the ranch. But everything inside of me resisted." Ed Mitchell was smart enough to notice that Paul was wavering after making the initial commitment, so Mitchell sent one of his people to stay with the Hastings for the two weeks before they left for the ranch. Paul continued to have grave doubts, but he was convinced that it was Satan trying to block him. "Now, as I look back, I think it was the Holy Spirit trying to say 'Hey, this is not of me at all.'"

Paul continued to resist the indoctrination process upon their arrival at the ranch. "It almost became a daily ritual where I'd get called 'on the carpet' one way or the other in what they call 'truth sessions.'" These sessions, which at first began with just a few persons, devolved into hostile verbal beatings before the entire group. Paul would be grilled, yelled and screamed at until he finally began yelling and screaming at himself and rebuking Satan.

Other members were also subjected to this "hot seat." Paul says, "To stay sane, you turn on other people. If you don't jump right in during the 'truth sessions,' and yell and scream as hard as the next guy—even though you don't know what in the world is going on—then you haven't 'supported' the group properly."

Three weeks after the Hastings committed themselves to the River of Life Ministries, Paul read newspaper accounts of a former member's death and the defection of ninety percent of Mitchell's following. The dead individual was a diabetic who had gone off his insulin after having been prayed over by River of Life members. He "stood by his healing," as did others in the group, regardless of his deteriorating condition, and consequently died. Most members left immediately after the tragedy; the few remaining loyalists were those who recruited the Hastings. As Mitchell began to see "persecutors" everywhere, Paul's indoctrination became even more difficult.

After the setback, because of the diabetic's death and the

loss of the majority of his following, Mitchell began to believe that a conspiracy against him had begun, consisting of all evangelical churches that had hundreds of airplanes and four-wheel drive vehicles at their disposal. He began sending groups of his followers to hide in the California desert. Paul notes: "The whole persecution thing, as I see it, is just a self-fulfilling prophecy. You do a bunch of off-the-wall, bizarre, crazy things, and sure, people are going to come after you and ask, 'Hey, what's going on here?' That's not persecution—not as Jesus experienced it."

In their desire to serve the Lord, the Hastings continued in River of Life and came increasingly under Mitchell's sway, primarily due to the constant barrage of guilt and spiritual hype. As MaryAnn indicates, "They have a public relations side...so warm and loving. And then there's the inner workings of the group, which included public humiliation and sometimes screaming sessions that would go on for two or three hours."

As the group deteriorated, these inner workings came to include physical abuse. "There was punching, hitting, children were whipped with belts, women were whipped with belts." This behavior was defined as "love" for the victim, because, "if you really love someone, then you're going to pay the price for that person to be set free. You're not going to compromise; you're going to confront them with their sin or their area of weakness and get them straightened out." Of course, the majority of this "love" came from Mitchell, who also constantly reminded the members how much he "suffered" by having to chastise the people and treat them the way he did. "He was always telling us how difficult it was for him to take all the steps that he took. And if you ever challenged him on anything, you wouldn't be challenging a human being, you'd be challenging the Holy Spirit because of his 'apostolic authority.'"

MaryAnn's experiences were even more traumatic than Paul's. Having been accused of being in league with the "evil spirit of Jezebel that controls every woman unless she is submitted to the spirit of God in her husband," MaryAnn was isolated from Paul and the children. She was dressed in "sackcloth and ashes" by Mitchell, called a seductress and a temptress, not allowed to bathe, forced to do heavy physical activity in the desert sun, and forced to confess that she had lustful desires for all the men and boys, including her own son. She was also accused of having a "spirit of mother-hood." This meant that she "idolized" her children and focused too much attention on them. "I was absolutely terrified to even talk to my children, show any kind of concern for them," even when her son fell and split his head open.

Eventually, because of the level of abuse, Paul and MaryAnn's children were taken from them, first by the Arizona Department of Public Social Services (at times the group moved around the Southwest quite a bit), and then, upon their return to California, by California authorities. The children were in foster homes for six months before MaryAnn left the River of Life Ministry. Paul left the following month with their oldest daughter, a teenager who did not leave willingly. "She was one of the ones Mitchell would surround himself with—certain people he knew could be manipulated. He just poured everything into these teenagers. They became even more valuable to him than the adults. And, it was an unwritten rule that one of their jobs was to report on their parents at all times."

Before their escape, Paul had been made president of the River of Life Corporation by Ed Mitchell. Mitchell told him, "Well, I've been freed of this; I want you to have this experience, Paul." Consequently, Paul would meet with the press to defend the group, talk with the attorneys, confront the sheriff's department—and shoulder all final fiscal re-sponsibility for the group. He is still being followed by bills that haven't been paid. As Paul says, "It was just a total set up. He used me because of my talents."

Paul, MaryAnn, and the children have put their lives back together in spite of the tremendous financial problems that Ed Mitchell and his River of Life Ministries left them. Paul says, "The Lord has really opened up a lot of doors for us. He found a school for me last year, kind of by accident, and now, in my second year, I can say without doubt that it is the nicest place I've ever been."

With his strong academic background in psychology and

years of experience, Paul gives this warning: "I've been involved with kids all of my life, dealing with different kinds of unusual behavior, and all that this experience says to me is that nobody is really immune; nobody is really safe from being sucked into something like this."

Virtually all authoritarian groups that I have studied impose discipline, in one form or another, on members. A common theme that I encountered during interviews with ex-members of these groups was that the discipline was often carried out in public—and involved ridicule and humiliation.

Discipline resulting from the infraction of rules or "failure to keep with the program," as well as "spiritual disciplines" imposed for one's spiritual betterment, have been reported by former members of the Community of Jesus, a controversial charismatic Christian group located in the Rock Harbor section of Orleans, Massachusetts, on Cape Cod. The Community of Jesus (COJ) exemplifies commitment to self-sacrifice and a semimonastic life-style in the context of what *The Christian Century* referred to as "tasteful affluence." The COJ accommodates resident members, associate members, and nonresident members, as well as the many middle- and upper-middle-class Christians who journey to the Cape each year to participate in retreats sponsored by the organization. Some of the evangelical notables who are associated with the Community include Peter Marshall, Jr., William Kanaga, who is Chairman of the Advisory Board of the New York firm Arthur Young, and at least one member of the Rockefeller family.

Two laypersons, Cay Andersen and Judy Sorensen, founded the Community around 1970 (Mrs. Andersen died several years ago). They soon became affectionately known as "Mother Cay" and "Mother Judy," and were at the center of the controversy that has swirled about the organization in recent years. In addition to what one churchman called its "lack of ecclesiology," the COJ has been accused of promoting a "theology of control" that focuses on attitudinal sins like jealousy, rebellion, willfulness, haughtiness, and idolatry. Critics and former members have argued that the Community has shifted toward an unbalanced, unbiblical, and highly structured program resulting in some people being abused emotionally and spiritually. There have also been reports of some forms of physical abuse. Media accounts, including an extensive article in *Boston* magazine, have aroused suspicions. These have been denounced by the COJ leadership.

According to a lengthy article appearing in the April 19, 1985 edition of the *Cape Codder*, former members stated that one of the cardinal sins at the COJ is to talk against Community disciplines in public. A group of ex-members have shared their concerns with reporters. "All of them had tales of being yelled and screamed at. All of them said they had been disciplined, in one way or another."

I have extensively interviewed a number of former members of the Community and have no reason to believe that they were being untruthful. Independent verification from various other sources has confirmed to me the questionable behaviors at the COJ, and has led me to include here a brief discussion of the problem. I do this despite repeated assertions to me by the leadership that the reports are invalid, and that they represent the complaints of only a handful of "disgruntled" ex-members. Several children of the founders have also departed the Cape and their leaving is dismissed by the leadership as a result of "family squabbles." It would seem that since reports of abuse continue to surface, to completely discount the experiences of these former adherents is to question the motives of an increasingly large group of people who have been, from their perspective, deeply hurt as a result of their association with the COJ. Because of its proximity to elements of the mainstream evangelical subculture, the Community of Jesus represents an unusual example of what many Christians, including many church leaders, see as a troublesome and unsettling phenomenon.

Since 1982, several presbyteries have initiated studies and critical assessments of the COJ, including the Presbytery of Boston and the Presbytery of Genesee Valley (NY). These

studies were undertaken because of the heavy involvement
of members and pastors of certain Presbyterian churches in
various COJ programs and retreats. In a report dated June
1987, the Synod of the Northeast concluded, among other
things, that "There is some evidence that in the use of
authority, some of the disciplines and practices of the
Community of Jesus have been appropriated by individuals
in less than helpful ways. The Agency [Synod Vocation
Agency] is particularly conscious of the authoritarian nature
of the Community of Jesus."

The comments of Don, an ex-member, demonstrate why
there is an uneasiness among many secular and Christian
observers regarding the Community. "While the leaders
continue to say that they don't *force* anybody to do anything,
there is such moral persuasion and such peer pressure that
there's no question that you would do whatever you were
expected to do. The alternative would be anything ranging
from a beating to being sent away from the Community,
which meant, separation from Jesus. None of us wanted that,
so therefore we would do what we were expected to do—not
because they stood over us with a whip, but because of the
psychological control they used in giving us the fear that we
would miss our calling or that we would be lost to Jesus if we
ever left."

Like members of other abusive groups, Don was led to
believe that he was joining an elite team. "We were often
told that there was no place in the world like the Community, that it was special." Don believes that many people
who join the Community have problems beforehand, or are
spiritually immature, and therefore vulnerable to manipulation. "People who were there all had reasons for joining.
Perhaps life was not going well for them, or they were
searching for something they couldn't find. By clever manipulation, the leadership convinced them that they could find
it at the Community. I was a new Christian, and they
convinced me that I would best find Jesus at the Community.
To leave the Community was to get out of God's will."

Don experienced firsthand the discipline that the Community administers. "I was told I talked too much. I was
directed not to speak more than three sentences at any one

time. And I had to wait until someone else had said something before I could say three more sentences. There were also dietary disciplines. One time we were all expected to go on a grape diet. For forty days we had grapes, grape juice, and raisins—that's all. A few were excused for medical reasons. But the great majority of us were expected to 'go on the grapes.'"

Don's wife was placed on what is known as the "silence discipline." She reports, "I was placed 'on silence' for six months, except for certain times when there was company in the house, or they decided I could be let off it, which wasn't very often. Once I had been sent to pull carrots and when I brought them back, I had, unfortunately for me, pulled up some small ones with the larger ones. I was verbally chastised for this and was told that I was not 'in the Spirit' and what did I have to say about it. They said I could speak and I fell into their trap; I began to defend myself and then I got another lambasting."

Don pointed out that no negative criticism of the Community was tolerated, a distinguishing feature of most totalitarian groups. "No one dared to say anything negative of any kind. I was actually afraid of being beaten up physically by members of the Community if I got out of line. No, you learned not to raise questions. We learned to keep our mouths shut. If someone questioned what the Community did, they were ridiculed and humiliated. That effectively shut up everybody else."

Members of the Two-by-Two's also experience the subtle effects of not making waves. "They struggle in vain to sort out what they believe, only to give up in frustration and confusion if they hope to survive. They are taught: 'When in doubt, do nothing,' 'do not question,' 'doubt is sin,' 'if you have a problem, go to more meetings,' and 'if you are unhappy, you need to count your blessings, sacrifice, suffer or submit more.' The resulting guilt, confusion, indecision, depression and low self-confidence become lifelong burdens one must bear in order to have hope of salvation."[1]

A former elder at Seattle's Community Chapel also discovered that you could not question the pastor. "The only way you can minister there is to stroke Don Barnett's ego. But once you cross him, that's it for you. There's no way that you can tell him that he's wrong. I flat out told him that what the church was involved in was sin, that it was an affront to a holy God. That was my demise as an elder."

In 1984 Pastor Barnett sent a memo about "Undermining the Pastor" to his elders and their wives. It read, in part, "I am alarmed to see a new trend which I believe the devil is in. A number of you to whom this letter is being sent have been privately sharing with others your personal opinions of how the pastor has given you wrong advice, the mistakes that we have made concerning revelations, and so forth. . . . To do this is to undermine the church; it is contrary to the church and the Word of God, and it is the devil's business. Those who are appointed to be representing the church have no business undermining the very church and pastor they represent, the one who has hired them to do their job. . . ."

Members of all abusive churches soon learn that the pastor or leader is beyond confrontation. As one former member of an abusive congregation put it, "Since no one in the church was allowed to murmur and complain, or to disagree with the pastor, there were many, like myself, who suffered in silence lest we incur God's anger." All problems that befall the group are the fault of members who violate the infallible rules. Accordingly, members experience increased self-doubt, helplessness, and insecurity.

> Oftentimes the deviant is barraged with attempts to get him to admit that he is guilty of crimes that he does not see. If he says that he is doubting the leadership, he has sinned because you are never to doubt the leadership. If he has talked to someone else about his concerns, he has sinned because you are never to plant "seeds of doubt" in others' minds about the leadership and/or the sect. If, however, the deviant does not agree with the definitions of his behavior that is placed by the group, he is immediately considered "unrepentant" and "unsubmissive."[2]

The ultimate form of discipline in authoritarian churches is excommunication or disfellowshipping, followed by strict avoidance procedures, or shunning. As MacDonald correctly notes, "Once the deviant is labeled as factious and is denounced, he is cast aside as thoroughly as one would throw out a dirty diaper. . .[the deviant] is no longer considered even to be an ex-member, but a wolf in sheep's clothing. He is referred to and looked to as how not to be."[3] When a rebellious individual leaves an abusive group, he is labeled as a traitor, a reprobate, a sinner, a backslider, or, in the case of Set Free Christian Fellowship, an "outlaw." The congregation is told to disassociate from such persons. "Friends of long standing will ignore him. They will turn their faces away. They will go to great lengths to avoid him. They will walk on the other side of the street, hang up the phone, or not answer the door. . . ."[4]

It is one thing to live through the devastation of an abusive-church environment. It is another thing to jump from the frying pan of one aberrant group into the fire of another abusive experience at the hands of one's supposed rescuer. Ed and Carolyn Roberts's story is another example of the very destructive and evil nature of abusive-church leadership.

Carolyn, the granddaughter of missionaries to Tibet, grew up in a very psychologically and physically abusive home. Her mother and stepfather had left by the time she was a teenager, and she moved in with her father and his wife at age sixteen. Feeling trapped in poverty and powerlessness, she turned to God and prayer. Carolyn believes that she was filled with the Holy Spirit and received the gift of tongues during this period of time.

At age eighteen, she went to work at a state mental hospital in California, but felt that God was calling her to Mexico. During a phone conversation in the middle of the night, she found out that her mother was going to Mexico to begin an orphanage. Believing that her termination from her job was a sign from God to go, she joined her mother who

promptly suggested that she attend a "school for discipleship" in Mexico. It was at this point, at nineteen years of age
and with very little Christian experience, that Carolyn
encountered Benjamin J. Hyde (not his real name) and
Witness to the World (not the actual name).

B. J. Hyde, fifty-six years old and blind, ran a small school
in Juárez, Mexico, where he was "training people to be
disciples and to become the bride of Christ." Carolyn admits
that she went there in part to get away from a young man
who was pursuing her. "I was so mixed up. I was having a lot
of problems with demonic spirits trying to make me think
that I was going to go crazy." Carolyn came from an abusive
family situation, and knew very little love, but the school
provided an environment of total love and acceptance. "It
just sucked me in." Of course, she did not see the real
dynamics of the group until much later.

Indoctrination began immediately. Being a rather stubborn individual, Carolyn would approach the woman in
charge of the disciples-in-training whenever she saw things
occurring that she did not agree with. She was told, "Well,
that's okay. Don't worry about it. God'll give you the
understanding of what is going on."

In time, Carolyn became one of seven women who were
supposed to be "spiritual wives" to B. J., as he was called.
She took a vow of celibacy and wore a ring that had "Jesus"
written in the center. She was to learn submission, humility,
and obedience through her special relationship with B. J. In
public circles, the "wives" were supposed to be wedded to
Jesus, but in the inner circle, they belonged to Hyde.

Hyde believed that the Lord had given him a new vision
and shown him a new thing. He was to prepare people for
the bride of Christ. Because he had "the mind of Christ," his
followers put on different garments according to the extent of
their humility. "When he deemed us humble enough, we
could put on another garment." The members were always
striving to be submissive, always working to be humble, and
always working to be acceptable in their leader's eyes. They
gave up all their worldly possessions to "apostle" B. J. Hyde,
whom they also affectionately called "Papa."

The group moved to El Paso where they had an "outreach" to servicemen, drug addicts, and runaways. It was at this "Lighthouse" that Carolyn began crying out to God, saying, "Lord, I cannot stand this anymore. I can't do this. I can't put up with this. He is such a mean, cruel man." People, like herself, with torn pasts and abusive histories, were the kinds attracted to Witness to the World. It was among the hurting and the unlearned that Hyde exercised his most abusive spiritual authority.

As a part of his "discipleship training," Hyde continually insulted his followers, because "we needed to learn submission, humility, and these were humbling things." Although he belittled, insulted, and berated the members, he would "respond to us with the right spirit if our spirit was right." Their spirits were rarely "right."

Ed, who joined the group a number of years after Carolyn, also became subjugated to Hyde. At first he thought that "Papa" Hyde and his seven dedicated spiritual wives were going to instruct and teach him in the ways of Jesus Christ. That's why he joined the little band. Now, in retrospect, he comments: "It's pretty amazing how a person can be drawn into such a group and be totally overcome and confused." Hyde would come across in the morning as sympathetic, constructive, benign, and benevolent. But by afternoon, if something had gone wrong or had not been carried out exactly the way he had intended, it would result in severe anger and chastening. Even when Hyde was clearly wrong, members got to the point of saying, "He's not at fault. I'm here because God has put me here, and he is going to refine and perfect me so that I will be ready when Jesus comes. So, I am going to humble myself under this absurd type of inquisition in order to purify my character weaknesses."

Hyde received the majority of his financial support from a woman named Emily Fuller, who, reportedly through some miraculous intervention and word, was shown that she was to give her substantial savings to him. Her on-going support, plus initial real estate investments, supplied Hyde and Witness to the World with sufficient funds for daily expenses. But members were put on food stamps. In addition, one of the "wives" worked as a secretary, and, if extra monies were needed for down payments on land or other purchases, members were sent to harvest tomatoes or do other menial work.

Regardless of one's position in Hyde's hierarchy, relations with family and close friends were cut off because "allegiance had to be to our spiritual family." Even though Carolyn was "third down on the list" of spiritual wives, under "Mother Superior" and "Mother Efficiency," there was no exception. When family members were questioned about their "worship" of Hyde, B. J. would respond: "They won't understand that all that is happening is God using me to perfect you and get you ready for the bride of Christ." The "bride of Christ" was supposed to be a very small number, only two out of every two million according to Hyde. Members were told that they would miss all the tribulation if they were willing to submit themselves as the bride of Christ now. "So we were willing to do anything to get ready to be right with the Lord." This included the loss of one's children.

Carolyn's sister joined the group two months after Carolyn, bringing with her an illegitimate baby who was just a few months old. "The baby was taken away from my sister and given to another woman. This is what he would do; he would break up the family like that." When Carolyn asked, "Why are you doing this?" he answered, "This bondage is not healthy. She has to look to me for everything, and this bondage between the mother and the son is too great. If she can't submit herself to me totally and allow me to do this with her child, then she's not totally submitted to the Lord." Carolyn laments, "It was pitiful because the little child was just thrown from one person to the next." Hyde also separated another family with four children, parceling out each child to one of his "spiritual wives."

Because of this and other incredible experiences, Carolyn began to balk at Hyde's authority. She became known as the "rebel" because she was constantly being chastised. Hyde would use the writings of William Branham, John Robert Stevens, and Lester Sumrall to support his positions, although he would not allow writings or teachings from more balanced perspectives to enter the group.

Carolyn, in her "rebellion," was subjected to physical

abuse as well. Hyde allegedly hit her and broke her
eardrum. He also put her on a total food and water fast
because she came to the aid of her nephew, whom Hyde was
tormenting. The cruelty increased upon their relocation to
Alabama. He would beat, or order the beating of, children
who wet their beds. He would not allow disciplined members to bathe for several weeks, and, because of Carolyn and
Ed's growing relationship, told Carolyn "to wash with my
tongue every place that I had stepped with Ed in my
'adulterous path.'" She was forced to clean the floor of
Hyde's very dirty trailer bathroom with her tongue because
she, as a "spiritual wife," had committed "spiritual adultery"
in her relationship with Ed. "I didn't want to go to hell," she
explained.

Eventually Witness to the World began to deteriorate. In
order to stop Joyce, Carolyn's sister, in her growing relationship with Dan, another man in the fellowship (dating was
considered demonic), Hyde sent her to a ministry run by
Phillip Benson. Carolyn had convinced him that Benson was
sympathetic to their "cause." There, she learned that Hyde
had allegedly engaged in unspeakable sexual conduct and
had had relations with a number of women in the group.
Carolyn, Ed, Joyce, Dan, and the majority of the rest of the
fellowship left Witness to the World upon hearing about
these allegations and went to Benson's camp on his invitation.

Benson performed the marriage ceremony for Carolyn and
Ed, as well as for Joyce and Dan. He also helped them set up
housekeeping. "We went to Bible study every day because
he said that we had to learn the Bible without this twisted
slant." However, Carolyn and Ed began to see that staying at
Benson's camp was in many ways similar to their experiences with B. J. Hyde. Benson claimed to have the same
"psychic abilities" as B. J. claimed to have. He told his
congregation that Ed was jealous of his "water witching"
skill. He attacked one of his members in front of the
congregation, bringing up his "past sins," because he
disagreed with Benson. Things did "not line up with the
Scripture." Ed and Carolyn began to see the exercise of

authority and the use of manipulation and abuse in this congregation as well.

Carolyn and Ed escaped and were later disfellowshipped from Benson's church. They were told that he told the others, "Don't pray for Carolyn and Ed anymore." He didn't want his church members "spending their spiritual energy" on them. Unfortunately, most of the ex-members of Witness to the World are still in Benson's camp, and they are now hostile toward the Roberts.

Carolyn and Ed have worked through their experiences with B. J. Hyde and Phillip Benson, and they have grown as Christians. Carolyn says, "I am not angry with God. I am not angry with Christ. I don't understand it all. I don't know how all of this fits, but I still trust him."

Ed adds, "I know that there is a lot of flexibility within the body of Christ and even in the theology of the church. I have tried to sharpen my senses to know what is on the 'outside' and what is on the 'inside.' I am more intense toward his Word and am a lot more protective of it, because when it is used properly, by the guidance of the Holy Spirit, it brings life and joy. When it is distorted, it's a monster."

———————————◆———————————

Unwavering obedience to religious leadership and unquestioning loyalty to the group would be less easily achieved if analysis and feedback were available to members from the outside. It is not without reason that leaders of abusive groups react so strongly and so defensively to any media criticism of their organizations. Don recalls what happened when adverse publicity about the Community of Jesus began to appear in the media. "We were told in a meeting by Mother Cay and Mother Judy that we were not to read the article in *Boston* magazine and the newspaper article because we didn't need to know about it. They said it was all baloney and that we were above all that sort of thing. We would stand for the persecution in the same way Jesus did." But then Don adds: "Some of us who were rebels *did* read it, and in our brainwashed state, swept under the rug a good bit of what was said. But I think it did lay some of the groundwork for later questioning."

In response to questions submitted by *The Cape Codder* to the Community of Jesus, the leadership issued a statement that essentially denied the allegations made by ex-members, claiming that the Community "stands in the long and honored tradition of monastic and semimonastic communities, which have existed since the early days of Christianity." Regarding the role of founders Cay and Judy, the statement said that members "certainly do not regard them as infallible or surrogates for God." The statement also made reference to Jesus' words, "By their fruits you shall know them." "We submit that the fruit of this Community's life can be seen in the incredible abundance of creativity—music, drama, art, crafts of every description, gardening, and writing (to name a few). . . ."[5]

Regarding the latter reference about being known by one's fruits, a former COJ member remarked to me, "The fruit of the Spirit is well outlined in Galatians chapter five and has nothing to do with gardens, music, drama, art, and crafts." Another ex-member, reacting to the statement, commented: "The leadership has done a beautiful job of putting together a large number of words that say nothing. They have never in any way responded directly to any of the facts which were stated as facts by various individuals in the media coverage. They always come out with a straw man that they set up and then batter down. 'Oh, we don't know of any of these things which the former members allege.' But they were *not* allegations, they were facts. We witnessed the events, we knew they took place, and they happened to *us*."

No one was more vociferous in his denunciation of the media than Hobart Freeman, pastor of Faith Assembly. Here is a sampling of his comments extracted from several of his sermons:

— "I don't care what the media says because it isn't true. It's 110% false."
— "The spirit of the anti-Christ is in the news media. N.E.W.S. means Negative Expression of What's Seen."
— "Your responsibility on behalf of this Body is no comment to the news media, *ever*!"

— "You're not obligated to answer one question to the media. They will turn everything you say against you."

— "When you feed information to the media, you're asking for persecution you don't need."

— "They don't know which end is up, spiritually, those religious reporters. Even when they try to report what they see, they can't see right. They're cross-eyed."

When authoritarian churches are subjected to what they perceive to be negative press, they invariably interpret the results as the "work of Satan." This is true even if the report appears in a Christian periodical, or when Christian observers are quoted.

I well remember the response of a columnist in the December, 1984 issue of *Charisma* magazine to a report authored by an *ad hoc* committee of evangelicals who had investigated allegations about Maranatha Christian Ministries. I was one of the authors of that report. We were all cast into the role of unwitting agents of Satan because we had critically evaluated Bob Weiner's organization. "How can one group of Christians be attacking a ministry which other respected leaders have called one of the most significant movements in America?" the columnist asked. The devil, he asserted, "attacks any vigorous expression of Christianity— by persecution and slander. . . ." He concluded his article by stating, "Wherever Maranatha is going in the future, I would like to go with them." I have often wondered how the columnist, seminary professor Richard Lovelace, felt a few years later when Maranatha was shut down as a ministry (to be discussed in chapter 11). Ironically, some of the reasons cited for Maranatha's demise were the very problems that we had identified in our report, which was so roundly denounced by Maranatha and others at the time of its release.

Criticism, whether its source is Christian or secular, sincere or superficial, is always viewed by fringe churches as an "attack"—and dismissed as more evidence of Satan trying to discredit "a good Christian work." In no way would I defend all that is passed off as investigative journalism aimed at Christian organizations. But I am aware of numerous instances where carefully researched, accurate reporting has been totally rejected by the evangelical Christian community without ever considering the possible merits of the reporting. It is almost automatically attributed to Satan. That is unconscionable.

A case in point involved the publication of an extensive journalistic investigation into Set Free Christian Fellowship, located in Anaheim, California. Following publication of the report in *The Orange County Register* on June 9, 1991, members of the Christian community appeared on the Trinity Broadcasting Network to denounce the article as an unjustified journalistic attack, a contrivance of the Adversary. Pastor Phil Aguilar was being interviewed and consoled by the hosts because of the "vicious persecution" he had endured at the hands of the press. The cohost made this incredible statement: "I've never read the article about you Phil, but I know that it's untrue." When Christians refuse to listen to "the other side," to say nothing of reading the material under discussion before commenting on it, they lose credibility with everyone. And let's not forget, there are almost always reasons why abusive organizations do not want exposure.

9

EXIT AND ADJUSTMENT
ABUSIVE CHURCHES
MAKE LEAVING PAINFUL

9

EXIT AND ADJUSTMENT
Abusive Churches
Make Leaving Painful

"I feel lost. I don't know where I'm going; I don't know
what I'm supposed to do; I don't know what I want; I don't
know who I am, and I want to know who I am. . .it was just
like one morning I woke up and collapsed. . . . I don't
understand why it seemed to work before, and why it's not
working now. There's a lot of confusion. . . . And I want to
tell you something about my husband—he's gone. There's
not anybody there in him—he's a void. He just can't
communicate. . . . A lot of my life's gone. . .a great portion of
it is gone. . . ."

As Beth Farrell described her exit process from Hobart
Freeman's Faith Assembly, it almost seemed as if she was
trying to retain her grip on sanity. Having lived for several
years almost entirely enveloped in Freeman's anti-intellectual, isolationist, name-it-and-claim-it subculture, she, her
husband, and their ten-year-old son were in agony as they
attempted to return to normal society and regain some sense
of themselves. Her son, having been born and raised in Faith
Assembly, has never known anything but spiritual legalism,
and, consistent with the group's beliefs, is deathly afraid of
physicians.

Hobart Freeman began Faith Assembly (not affiliated with
the Assemblies of God) after both his dismissal from the
faculty of Grace Theological Seminary and his excommunication from the Grace Brethren Church in Indiana in 1963.
Holding a doctorate in Old Testament Theology and

169

Hebrew, Freeman was a successful minister of a large congregation and the author of several books. However, he held some variant positions on doctrine and practice that became increasingly extreme over the years.

Of greatest significance was Freeman's position on medicine and physicians. He referred to doctors as "medical deities" and claimed that medicines had demonic names and, if taken, opened one up to demonic influence. Members of Faith Assembly were, and still are, strongly discouraged from seeking medical attention for any maladies suffered. As a result, at least ninety persons of Faith Assembly have died of preventable and treatable illnesses. One report indicates that the church has averaged about one preventable death per month since 1978. These deaths include forty-two infants, ten children between the ages of one and seventeen, seven mothers who died of complications related to home births, and numerous adults who suffered illnesses that were inadequately treated.

According to Freeman's "faith-formula theology," God is obligated to heal every sickness if a believer's faith is genuine—so that Faith Assembly members felt they could actually avoid death. After a "positive confession" is made concerning the healing, symptoms of illness or injury that remain are viewed as deception from the Devil. If death occurs in spite of this positive confession, it is seen as either discipline from God or a lack of faith, or even, as in Job's case, a testing of faith. Freeman himself died of severe cardiovascular disease and mild bronchopneumonia in 1984, an embarrassment to his church. No Faith Assembly folks attended his burial. Leadership has been passed on to his sons-in-law.

Although Faith Assembly is most noted for its positive-confession approach to healing, where believers must "claim" healing by acknowledging that it has taken place before any indication of the fact, its members also follow a number of other questionable doctrines and practices. They are discouraged from reading newspapers, watching television, and meeting with members of other churches. They buy no insurance, wear neither glasses nor contact lenses, and remove the seat belts from their cars, preferring to "live by faith alone." Wives are expected to be submissive, obedient homemakers who practice no birth control. All members are to put the "Body" first and their familial relationships second (Beth's own husband and another Faith Assembly elder caused her to be disfellowshipped— shunned—for months). Higher education is strongly discouraged, and, because most members give the bulk of their income to the church, they live in relative poverty—in contrast to the allegedly wealthy life-styles of Faith Assembly leaders.

Celebrations of Christmas and Easter, considered pagan customs, are forbidden. Freeman's teachings are to be accepted without question, no matter how twisted the scriptural basis. To question Freeman, a self-acknowledged "prophet of God," is to risk the charge of blasphemy. Since Freeman believed that the Trinitarian formula of Matthew 28:19 is improper, although he held to a traditional, orthodox view of the Trinity, members are baptized in the name of Jesus only. Members are told to pray only once concerning a matter to avoid "vain repetition." Married individuals should not have sexual foreplay, or sex for pleasure, so as to avoid inciting "lust." Members are not to swear any oaths in a court of law, and they are prohibited from consulting attorneys.

This is only a sampling of the types of strictures under which Faith Assembly members live, but, looming above them all, is the constant need to have a "positive confession." "We were taught to practice thought control. . .to deliberately empty our minds of everything negative concerning the person, problem, or situation confronting us."

Out of this maelstrom stepped Beth and her family. Already having experienced the pain of the break up of their house fellowship in 1975, they are now devastated by this most recent event in their pursuit of faith. Ten years of study and work had enabled them to become leaders and teachers in Faith Assembly. They learned Hebrew and Greek for Bible study and a whole theological system interpreted according to Freeman's personal beliefs. Having left Freeman's fold, they were in a quandary. No other fellowship of Christians could possibly measure up. Other believers do not show the same sincerity and seriousness about their faith. Consequently, Beth and her family do not know where to go. The mainline denominational structure is what drove them to an informal home fellowship and then to Faith Assembly in the first place. However, they realize there is no going back to a group where dead newborn babies are secretly buried by their parents for fear that the "Body" will find out and their lack of faith become evident to all.

Beth had never been able to attain "the faith" as did her Faith Assembly leader models, and therefore she was unable to garner the benefits of a fulfilled life. Even though at the beginning of their involvement, she and her family would buy Freeman's tapes and books before they would buy food, her zeal never measured up to the standard. At this point she feels as if she is "leaving the truth...leaving the Word of God...leaving everything, and there's no Christianity outside. I guess that's why I feel lost. I don't know where I'm going; I don't know who I am."

Beth now feels extremely guilty for having minor surgery, for getting contact lenses as soon as she left Faith Assembly, and for being "sentimental" about her son. In Faith Assembly, showing strong affection and protectiveness toward one's children is tantamount to idolatry. She feels guilt because of the number of physical ailments her son has had to suffer over the years—without treatment—and for the fact that he has never visited a dentist. She harbors guilt for feeling angry toward the Faith Assembly leaders and toward herself, and most especially for having left the only anointed work of God on earth.

Unfortunately, not only is guilt a terrible burden, but there is a lack of trust toward anyone who is a religious authority figure. Having been leaders and teachers in Faith Assembly, Beth and her husband now have no one to turn to for guidance and support. All of their significant relationships of the past years are still within the group. Who counsels the counselors? Beth wants to speak with someone who is "safe," but she is unable to trust her own abilities of discernment and evaluation since they were so long labeled as unspiritual. Consequently, she says she "goes into these periods where all I'll do is feel like I've died."

Beth's husband is also having great difficulties. Although capable of functioning at work, all emotional moorings are gone in other aspects of his life. He and Beth have very little relationship, and he has lost what she terms "aspects of his personality." No longer having a context in which to place himself outside of his work, he is emotionally isolated and unable to sort out his experiences with Faith Assembly. He is in shock.

Beth's son is also having a hard time. The context of his entire life has changed. Having grown up within Faith Assembly, nothing is familiar or comfortable now. He had to have all of his childhood shots in order to enter the sixth grade at a public school and went into hysterics during his first physical examination. He refuses to take vitamins or medications, and has had great difficulty socializing at school. Because his parents are still emotionally unstable, he has a tenuous and shaky home life. Many childhood ailments, including a broken foot, have gone untreated and are still in need of attention.

Beth, having stifled all of her maternal affections over the past ten years, is not even sure if she knows how to love her son. Within Faith Assembly, she says, "your children are under subjection to you and you teach them that. If they don't submit [appropriately]. . .if you don't take care of your children, then the church will. . . .   It breaks you all up!" Beth is confused about how to raise her son within a new and entirely different world—the world outside of Faith Assembly.

Beneath the insecurities of all the sociological and psychological changes that Beth and her family have experienced are the shaky underpinnings of a faith in God that is no longer firmly anchored. Theology, doctrine, and works have been ends in themselves over the past years. Although the Faith Assembly motto is "God is faithful," the outworkings of that motto required an unswerving and unquestioning obedience to Freeman's doctrines and beliefs. Members, not God, were required to be faithful. So the "overcomers" and "manifested sons of God" of whom Beth and her family were supposed to be a part, have experienced neither freedom in

Christ nor liberation from the oppressive works-not-grace orientation.

Restoration, after experiencing the effects of an abusive-church situation, can be a long and painful process. This can be true even if the exposure to that influence was only of short duration. Individuals have even been devastated after only a few short months. Much assistance from family, friends, and the church is needed.

Beth and her family were for over ten years exposed to toxic faith—the sort of abusive religion that made them sick. But now they are beginning to receive the help that they need. They are rebuilding relationships and addressing such practical issues as insurance and health care. And they are in the process of finding God again—in a new and different light.

As one can see from Beth's case, leaving an abusive-church situation can be extremely difficult, calling into question every aspect of life members may have experienced for the period of time they were involved. I want to discuss the range of emotions and issues that ex-members may face when they exit an abusive-church situation. Then I will provide a general overview of the changing experiences, feelings, and needs that emerge over the course of weeks, months, and even years after departure.

Leaving a restricted and abusive community involves what sociologists call the *desocialization* process whereby the individual loses identification with the past group and moves toward *resocialization,* or reintegration into the mainstream culture. There are a number of emotions and needs that emerge during this transition process. How one deals with these feelings and affective experiences has a significant impact on the overall healing that is required.

Many have described the aftermath of abusive-church involvement as comparable to that of rape victims, or the delayed stress syndrome experienced by war veterans. It is recovery from what might be called spiritual rape. You feel like something has been lost and you will never be the same again.

Initially, victims may have a total lack of feeling regarding their experience. They may not evidence pain, anger, sadness, or even joy at being free. Such lack of feeling may be a protective mechanism from the strong surge of emotion that is sure to come. Victims need a safe and secure environment in which to vent their emotions. Such venting was often labeled as "sin" in their previous environments, and it may take some time until they give themselves permission to allow these feelings to surface.

Whether or not they show any emotion, victims are in great need of empathetic, objective individuals who will not treat them like spiritual pariahs or paranoid storytellers. The events they have just been through are as unbelievable to them as they are to their listeners. They have experienced great social and psychological dislocation. An open attitude on the part of friends, family, and counselors greatly assists the healing process.

Feelings of fatigue are common among people when they first disengage. It is not unusual for them to need to sleep for long periods. As one former member recalls, "Emotionally drained, I was often physically impaired. . . . As a result, it was sometimes difficult for me to function. . . . I was frequently emotionally unavailable to my husband and children, and much of the time I simply wanted to be left alone."

Victims are extremely vulnerable at this point. They have come out of an all-embracing religious environment where there are no grays, only blacks and whites. While members of authoritarian groups, they have had to put aside their old relational and coping styles and learn the ones acceptable to the group. Often these are antisocial and confrontational. And coming out of a context where they developed strong dependency needs, they are extremely suggestible and vulnerable to those whom they feel they can trust, whether counselor, immediate family member, or pastor. Betraying that trust can wreak havoc on them, only validating the warnings of their previous leader concerning the "outside world," and perhaps driving them back into another (or even the same) regimented environment where they feel they can at least control some of the variables. Lack of control can be terrifying.

Having been in an environment that frequently includes spiritual manipulation, emphasis on experience, and focus on demons, victims of abusive churches may experience a lack of reality upon leaving the group. They may believe that they can easily pick up where they left off before entering the group, regardless of the changes in the larger society and in their friends and family. They soon discover that reentry does not involve simply returning to one's previous life-style. In short, they can't go home. The future may appear to be unrealistically bright or ominous, depending on the condition in which the person reentered the mainstream. As one ex-member of the Church of the Great Shepherd states, "It is an extremely important factor whether a person leaves an abusive-church situation knowing that the group was wrong, or believing that *he* was wrong and is now sinning against God."

Vague and undefined anger is common at this point. Victims may be easily upset and frustrated, yet they have no focus for their anger. They may also be strongly repelled or fascinated by spiritual issues, either completely rejecting or consuming literature that might explain and give reasons for the ordeal they underwent.

A letter I received from a woman in the midwest describes some of these feelings. "It's only been a year since we've left and there are days when I still feel I have had the air punched out of me. The cult books really don't address the issue that I find hardest to reconcile: I can't dismiss these people completely because, while they are 'cultic' in terms of psychological control, they still claim Christian doctrine and therefore they are still my brothers and sisters in Christ."

Feelings of isolation can be devastating, especially for those who have walked out of abusive churches on their own without any support. Victims may feel a sinking sense of loss and be unable to relate to other people, even in the midst of a crowd. They are lonely and alone. Very few can understand what they have been through. As one woman describes it, "The complexity of the experience is so great that it is impossible to adequately communicate it to someone who has not gone through it." Vietnam veterans have expressed very similar feelings.

If the group from which they defected was tightly structured, and the victims have cut off all previous ties to friends and family, they may come out into the real, cold world without any support systems whatsoever. Consequently, they may have great difficulty trusting those with whom they have no history. They have left behind their best friends, their spiritual family, with whom they have shared intimate, daily experiences for years. Those same friends now shun them and treat them as enemies and traitors. Without help, victims may become suicidal or severely ill, either physically or mentally. Depression is almost inevitable.

As one ex-member of a small, East coast church stated, "When I left the group, I experienced hell. I felt an unbearable separation from God. I felt that God had left me, that I was divorced from someone I was deeply in love with. My whole life was over. I felt like a floating cloud. I felt extreme guilt over leaving my 'family' and betraying those I loved. I felt that God would kill me. . . . I used to take long drives and just scream as loud as I could, the pain and the guilt were unbearable."

It is possible, though difficult, to come through such an experience without a support system of any kind. However, victims who have not had the opportunity through a support system to sort through their varied emotions, thoughts, and spiritual confusion, may end up with deep, unresolved hurts. The development of a new social-support structure, therefore, is crucial.

I have had the opportunity to follow the progress of one young woman who left an abusive-church group on her own. She has finally reached a point where she understands what happened to her, but it has taken her several years to sort it all out. "The majority of my recovery took four years," she writes. "It took me two and a half years of continual searching for the truth, gradual healing, encouragement, reading the Bible, and spending much time alone with God before I was healed and renewed in my mind enough to face the fact that I had been deceived. The mental, emotional, and spiritual hold that the group had on me was not broken until I personally renounced them and divorced myself from them. It took two and a half years to be ready to do that.

"When I did, I was able to see that they had gradually become my God and took the place of my relationship with him. It was so painful to face the truth. I remember feeling like God was watching me and longing for me while I was pouring out my love on someone else. I'm so glad that he never left me, but was waiting the entire time for me to come back to him even though I was convinced while in the group that I was serving him with my whole heart."

Every person exiting an abusive-church situation has a different story to tell, and they have differing needs and emotions. The immediate post-involvement phase may last for weeks or months, depending on the trauma experienced and the amount of assistance received. Although there are no clear-cut boundaries between one wave of experiences and emotions and the next, ex-members soon begin to have a secondary set of issues to deal with, particularly as reality begins to set in.

The real world of conflict, bills, crime, diapers, in-laws, auto repairs, and employment may have been very far removed from some victims. Upon their return to life in the "real world," defectors will experience a variety of emotions—the strongest being depression, frustration, and alienation. The world often appears to be cold and uncaring.

Individuals exiting after a span of years may come out in completely different life contexts, bringing with them an entirely different set of experiences and values. Single persons may exit married, or, conversely, married persons may leave divorced. Couples may exit with children, some of whom may be damaged because of exposure to the group. Parents may have no idea how to care for their children. They have guilt feelings over holidays missed, birthdays overlooked. There is a mourning over lost years, and a desire to return to life-as-it-was. One ex-member, reflecting on Joel 2:25, told me that he would pray, "Lord, return those wasted years."

Along with the need to recapture the past and rebuild relationships, the ex-member experiences a growing level of anger, frustration, and powerlessness. The vague anger associated with first leaving becomes more focused and intense. There may be strong desires for revenge along with guilt and self-condemnation for having such feelings. The frustration and powerlessness of knowing that one has been taken advantage of, and the awareness that there is little that can be done about it, are very difficult emotions to handle.

Questioning one's past experiences also becomes more acute. Victims begin to experience guilt over a variety of issues. How could I have let this happen to me? How could I have treated my parents that way? Have I really left the Lord? Am I in sin and committing blasphemy at this moment? How could I have let my children be so abused? What's wrong with me? Was it really *all* wrong?

Alternatively, ex-members may assume a posture of avoidance, desiring to retreat from their painful experiences in the group and wanting to maintain a certain level of anonymity in their life circumstances. They are not yet ready to handle all of the issues that seem to be assaulting them. They do not question the past, and they prefer to lose themselves in harmless and engrossing diversions like sports, shopping, crafts, novels, and games.

If they have been able to maintain employment independent of the group, ex-members might use their careers as anchors, something in their lives that has not been turned upside down. They will throw themselves into their work with abandon, getting "lost" in their jobs for a period of time in order to sort out the many problems of transition. Some will seek an entirely new identity by acquiring a new occupation with its attendant opportunities to gain new friends.

During this phase, professional or pastoral counseling can be of great benefit. Victims begin experiencing a growing awareness of their own needs. They are not as confused as when first exiting, and may very well be in need of more than just a listening ear. Complicated issues need to be addressed and worked through. Relationships are in need of repair. A safe environment is essential for venting their feelings, doubts, and questions. Therapists who blame them for their involvement in the abusive-church situation, or, who attempt to focus on the dysfunction that led to their victimization, may hinder the process of reintegration.

I have found that individuals often experience great embarrassment at being so "taken in" by the leader of the group, and for acting so foolishly during their time of membership. A Baptist pastor from Massachusetts, the Reverend James Wood, has counseled at least twenty former members of the Community of Jesus; he has noticed the same phenomenon. "There is also a sense of shame, an embarrassment for the things they allowed themselves to be manipulated into doing." Reverend Wood also observes that ex-members have a difficult time committing themselves to anything again. "They feel betrayed. Their commitment was abused and now they are reluctant to commit again."[1]

A caring and competent counselor can help sort through these post-involvement feelings, as well as the anger, frustration, and depression. It is important for the counselor to keep in mind that the decision to join probably came out of a sincere desire to love and serve God.

However, the ex-member may very well be doubting the existence of God at this point, and may have focused his or her anger at God. People should be permitted to express that anger. They may also be ambivalent about their past commitments and have mixed feelings about their past membership. One former member described a canopy of diverse feelings during this phase of her readjustment, including "intense humiliation, guilt for leaving loved ones, condemnation, hopelessness, confusion, fear, lack of purpose for living, deep depression and despair, distrust of other Christians, abandonment, and betrayal by God."

The experience of a former member of the communal Emmaus Christian Fellowship in rural Colorado illustrates many of these feelings and is typical of the many accounts I have documented in various groups during years of research. "Two of the elders yelled at and talked to me for four hours," she reports. "I was told I was a stubborn, rebellious woman, that I was throwing away my salvation, hanging onto pagan holidays [Christmas and Easter], and wanting my boy to play baseball." One elder also told her "that when he stood before Jesus Christ on Judgment day, he would tell Jesus that I didn't really want to make it to the kingdom of heaven."

Like so many of the ex-members of spiritually abusive groups that I have interviewed, this woman left with a heavy load of guilt, somehow feeling that she was to blame and at fault for what had transpired. "I doubted my salvation. I had lost all my best friends whom I had shared my life with for five years. I was literally devastated. I was pregnant at the time, and I lived in mortal fear that something would be wrong with the baby, that God had cursed me and my child."

This woman lived in a very small town. Following her departure from the group, she found it difficult at first to confront her former church members in public. "I just couldn't face anyone. I dreaded going to the post office or the store, afraid I would run into someone." Then, when she was able to reach out to them, her efforts were rebuffed, "with either excuses or by their outright ignoring me." The reason: "I had broken covenant. I had turned my back on God. I was the worst kind of heathen there was. I was lost and there was no hope for me in their eyes."

As we have already seen, this kind of spiritual intimidation was also commonly used in Maranatha Christian Churches. "If you leave without the leadership's approval," states one former Maranatha member, "condemnation and guilt are heaped upon you. My pastor told me he thought it was satanic for me to leave and he wondered whether I could continue in my salvation experience." This kind of teaching was used as spiritual leverage to keep people in the church.

In a now-defunct ultra fundamentalist group in California, members were informed in writing of the *only* acceptable way to leave their church and remain "in God's will":

"1. Pray about the matter alone for three months (husbands and wives only may consult each other during this period).

2. Bring the matter to the superintendent and leaders for their guidance. They will pray over the matter for another period of one to three months. (You are not to mention your desire to leave to anyone other than your husband or wife during this period as well).

3. You must abide by the decision of the leaders whether to leave or not at the end of their deliberation."

As one former member of this organization commented to me, "Why bother to pray; the leaders make the final decision in any event."

Former members of extremist Christian churches often compare the process of leaving to marital separation. As one ex-member of a church in the South describes it: "We who left were labeled 'rebels against God' and cut off from fellowship with those who remained, those we had worshiped, worked, and prayed with as a close-knit family for five years. It was like a divorce."

In writing about Great Commission International (GCI), an organization founded in 1970 by "apostle" Jim McCotter, former member Jerry MacDonald notes that the group compares its leadership structure with a marriage. "GCI elders frequently refer to ones that have left the church as *divorcing* themselves from their family. They twist Scripture on God's hatred of divorce and use it as a coercive technique to keep people from leaving their churches. Thus, ones who leave are taught that they have actually left God and sinned. What it really means is that the elders have usurped the loyalty and the devotion that is due Christ alone and refocused it on themselves."[2]

MacDonald points out that the proof-text for the idea of "marriage" in relation to elders and leaders in GCI is found in Ephesians 5:22–6:9. The group cites 5:22 ("Wives, submit to your husbands as to the Lord") as the key to their hierarchical system of authority. "Just as wives are to be in subjection to their husbands, so the church is to be in subjection to the elders. It seems that the elders are the physical manifestation of the authority of Christ. Just as a family mirrors the church's relationship to the elders, so a wife and husband in the bond of marriage reflect the subjection the congregation should have to the elders."[3]

In the Great Commission International, much emphasis is placed on "trusting God's leading through others"—the "others" being those in leadership. In reality, this means surrendering one's independence, obeying in all things, and submitting to the leaders. As numerous ex-members of GCI have told me, it amounts to the subjugation of members to the leadership. Failure to comply with the authoritarian dictates of the group can result in ex-communication, a common practice in GCI and other abusive-church groups.

> If you do not give up your independence and follow in harmony, you will be reproved for "sowing discord in the body," and if you still do not "harmonize," you will be excommunicated for faction—since, according to GCI, there is no difference between trusting God and trusting a GCI leader.[4]

As I have noted elsewhere in this book, excommunication is almost always accompanied by shunning behavior instituted by the leadership. For example, whenever members were disfellowshipped from Community Chapel in Seattle (and that was a regular occurrence), this action was mentioned in the Sunday bulletin. "The pastor requests that members of our congregation have no further contact with [names of the persons involved are listed]; they have been disfellowshipped from this church. Do not call them for advice or ask their opinion about spiritual and soulical [Pastor Barnett's own term, equivalent to "fleshly"] relationships, the church leadership, or any other matter. If they call you, politely hang up as quickly as possible. These people are not—and never have been—in a position to give direction or advice regarding the move of God in our church. Your cooperation in this matter will help you, and is greatly appreciated by the pastor."

One need not have psychological training to understand that such a procedure also operates as an effective control mechanism within a church. Those who are the "boat-rockers," those who raise uncomfortable questions and who challenge the leadership in any way, are prevented from sharing their legitimate concerns and criticism with other members. Dissent is muffled, and disinformation can be "spiritualized" or manipulated by the leadership.

Even while admitting how badly they have been treated by an abusive church, former members may vacillate between rejecting the past and defending the group they have

left. In the latter instance, they may feel like they are
betraying their old "spiritual family." Many times while
talking with ex-members I have heard them speak positively
about the close, interpersonal ties that they developed while
in the group and how difficult it is to recreate that intimacy
on the outside. Or they defend the worship style of the
group.

Another common response I have noticed among former
members is the feeling that they were alone in their
struggle—even thinking they were perhaps "a little crazy"
for having had such experiences. "Am I the only one to have
experienced this kind of thing?" many would ask. Discover-
ing a published article on the phenomenon has also
benefitted some victims greatly because they realize that
they are not alone. Even more effective is encountering
someone who has experienced the same abuse. "There is
actually someone else out there like me who understands!"

The best persons to reach out to church abuse victims are
former victims. As one ex-member puts it, "The two main
things that helped me more than anything were reading the
Bible frequently and talking to people who had had similar
experiences." I am aware of several informal support groups
that have formed to serve the needs of individuals leaving
specific organizations. The Wellspring Retreat and Resource
Center in Albany, Ohio, is a unique, residential counseling
facility that provides professional assistance to victims of
spiritual abuse. Its capable director, Dr. Paul R. Martin,
psychologist and evangelical Christian, was once a member
of Great Commission International (GCI), an organization
mentioned in this book.

It may take victims years to sort out experiences, begin to
make definitive choices for themselves, and reach a point of
full integration into the mainstream culture. This is especially true if they have received no support or assistance.
One ex-member reports, "During the first year after leaving,
all I did was hide from everyone. I grew a beard and a
moustache, let my hair grow long, and took nondescript, low-
paying jobs. I didn't see my parents, my brother, no one.
And, I thought God was going to kill me.

"The second year, I planned on leaving for Alaska, but

then a job dropped into my lap, and I took it. I started looking around for a church to attend, but I just couldn't take it. I moved into my friend's garage, remodeled it, and just lived day-to-day.

"This is my third year out, and I feel like I can finally look back on the experience and say that God is using it to teach me wisdom about the world. I know that God is not condemning me and I can go on. I am attending a church now, have made some new friends, and feel like I can live again."

Even as victims begin to assimilate their abusive experiences and adjust to normal life, certain problems may persist, stemming from the programming they experienced while in the group. There may be difficulty relating to supervisory personnel in the workplace. Understandably, religious authority figures represent a major source of uneasiness on the long road back. Victims may also have difficulty trusting new friends, workmates, and acquaintances, all the while feeling guilty for having a judgmental attitude. There may be deep fears—abandonment by a spouse, death of one's children, or never again having a date—that are triggered by certain circumstances. Additionally, healing may need to occur between victims, friends, and family, including spouses who were pitted against one another by the church leader, children who verbally abused their parents, and friends who were rejected when they expressed concern.

As confidence grows and decisions become easier to make, the reawakening of spiritual needs and desires will occur. After months or years apart from conventional Christianity, former members may again want to ask questions like, What does it mean to love God with all my heart, soul, mind, and strength? How do I love God more than my own life? Can I really live out discipleship without being hurt again? Can I share all things in common with others and not be part of an abusive church?

The idealism and zeal for God that initially drove these persons into abusive-church situations is now coupled with insights on distorted spirituality and human manipulation that is more than academic. They feel "wiser for the experience." However, a benign naïvete on the part of both

old and potentially new friends regarding spiritually abusive
churches often makes it difficult to establish understanding
relationships. By this I mean that ex-members often sense
that they are the objects of uncertain acceptance when they
try to share what they have been through. Unstated though
clearly communicated sentiments like, "There had to have
been something wrong with you to get involved in a church
like that," can be a real discouragement to those hoping to
regain normalcy.

A bit of advice for those of us who have been fortunate
enough to avoid any experience of spiritual abuse: When you
encounter someone from an authoritarian church background, listen to them with an open mind, and don't
perpetuate unkind stereotypes. Above all, they need our love
and acceptance.

10

DISCERNMENT AND RESPONSE
ABUSIVE CHURCHES PRESENT A WARNING

10

DISCERNMENT AND RESPONSE
Abusive Churches Present a Warning

A central theme of this book is that spiritual abuse can take place in the context of doctrinally sound, Bible preaching, fundamental, conservative Christianity. All that is needed for abuse is a pastor accountable to no one and therefore beyond confrontation. Witness Bonnie Mason's fifteen-year experience in Midvale Bible Church (not the church's actual name), an independent, Midwestern, Baptist-oriented church with a pulpit-thumping, fire-and-brimstone preaching, fundamentalistic pastor who believed himself to be beyond question—until the day he died, which was the day Bonnie and her family were freed.

Bonnie and Keith Mason came to know the Lord the day before they met Pastor Carl Plummer (the names of the pastor and his wife are pseudonyms). Although Keith had been raised in a Christian home, he had never made a commitment of faith and had spent his years becoming an accomplished rock musician. Bonnie, on the other hand, had had no exposure to Christianity whatsoever. Together they saw a Christian film so powerful in its impact that they wanted to commit their lives to Jesus Christ. The next day, on advice from friends, they called Carl, a new pastor in town. He came over immediately, and the Masons received Jesus as their Lord and Savior.

Keith immediately asked Carl if he thought he should quit his career in music. Although Carl never came out and openly stated that Keith's career was ungodly, Keith felt from his statements that to remain in rock music would be to somehow "compromise his witness." Keith gave in to Carl's oblique suggestions and counsel. This type of indirect "wisdom" from Carl was to control the Masons' lives for the next fifteen years.

Bonnie fell completely under Carl's influence. She felt she had been saved by Pastor Carl Plummer, and she began looking up to him as a father figure, one who could answer all of her questions about her new life. Carl responded, again with oblique comments, expressing general "concerns," preaching in pointed generalities from the pulpit, so that, without ever having to say so directly, he communicated to Bonnie, and to others, that his way of doing things was the right and godly way. Bonnie was never taught that there is diversity in the body of Christ, that differences of opinion are allowable and healthy, and that one can follow the Lord in a number of different contexts and different churches. This "missing ingredient," as Bonnie calls it, kept her doubting herself and in literal slavery to Carl and his family until he died.

A wall began to form between Bonnie and Keith as they became more and more involved in the church in which Carl was serving as pastor. On one hand, Carl would tell Bonnie to love and obey her husband. On the other hand, Bonnie knew that if Keith did not do things exactly as Carl did them, he was obviously not being committed to God. He ought to be living his life exactly like Carl. The distance between them widened when the church split and Pastor Carl took those loyal to him to form Midvale Bible Church. Although Keith protested, Bonnie convinced him to go along. Up to that point, Carl Plummer had not served in any given church for more than two years without leaving for one reason or another.

From the beginning, Carl preached on submission to authority. He told his people that a pastor is responsible to speak for God and should not be questioned. As their pastor, he was extremely burdened because of the sins of God's people, and, when he fell ill from heart disease, he told them that it was their responsibility because of the great load he bore for them before God. Over time, this guilt and pressure mounted to intolerable levels.

During the first few years, Midvale met in a series of motels and homes, never constructing a building of their own. Meanwhile, the Plummers were given a large parsonage on six acres. At this point, three years into this ministry, Carl began rebuking the women of the congregation from the pulpit for not befriending and reaching out to his wife, Eileen. Why had they not been meeting with her? Why had they not asked her to go shopping?

Bonnie, by this time fully under Carl's influence, responded immediately. Up till now, she had been emulating Eileen and her children in every respect. Since Eileen wore no makeup or earrings, neither did Bonnie. Since her children wore a particular brand of clothing and had their hair styled a particular way (even though they were years older than Bonnie's kids), Bonnie had her children dressed and coiffed in like manner. Now the opportunity had arisen to do an even more godly thing. She began taking Eileen shopping (Eileen couldn't drive). And, she even begged the Plummers to allow her to help clean their home when they knew that Eileen's sister was coming to visit. The Plummers had been so good to her, had instructed her in the faith, and helped her to grow as a Christian. It was the least she could do.

This was the beginning of Bonnie's becoming the "handmaid" to Eileen Plummer and her family. The onetime assistance grew into a daily ritual. She began to deceive her husband, who knew nothing of the extent of her bondage. Bonnie would go over to the Plummer's home at 11:30 A.M. and arrive back home in time to prepare dinner and meet Keith at the door. Her children became "latchkey kids," since Mom was away taking care of the Plummer children. Keith knew nothing, and Bonnie believed that she was serving God. She felt she was working out her salvation because she was not loving "son or daughter more than me. . ." (Matt. 10:37). To be enslaved to the Plummer family was to love God.

Meanwhile, because the children were getting older and because money was getting tight, Keith began talking to

Bonnie about going to work to supplement their income. However, Carl would speak to her about how much her children needed her at home, even while knowing that she was at *his* house, caring for *his* children. He would praise her from the pulpit, holding her up as an example of servanthood.

Bonnie's confusion grew, and she began crying out to God each day, praying that Eileen would not have another task for her to carry out. She wondered why other women, with fewer responsibilities at home, were not offering assistance. She found out that two others *had* offered, but were turned down by Eileen, saying "Bonnie will do it." Her reputed example of spirituality caused the other women of the church to hate and envy her. Meanwhile, she was in emotional agony.

Bonnie felt that she had to confide in Carl Plummer about every aspect of her life. Using Psalm 51, Carl had preached that not exposing one's sins to the world was trying to hide them from God. Consequently, Bonnie told all, including the most intimate details of her life. She knew that she had already told God herself, but Carl never said she didn't need an intermediary.

When Bonnie's father was dying of cancer, she felt guilty when she would take time to go see him, only fifty miles away. She felt that she was putting her father before God, and putting her family's interests before her commitment to the Lord. Plummer did nothing to discourage such thinking. She knew it was a sin to visit her father on Sunday, and she asked her pastor if he would go visit him. He refused, saying he didn't want to infringe on another pastor's territory. When her father died, the Plummers comforted her by telling her to come back and throw herself into servanthood. It would be the best therapy for her.

Bonnie became so confused that she stopped wanting to follow Carl Plummer, no longer wanted to listen to him preach, and stopped wanting to attend the mandatory meetings—even though she knew she would be castigated from the pulpit for lack of commitment. She began to realize that there was no consistency in what Carl taught. Why did he allow women to get permanents but not color their hair?

Why did he allow necklaces and finger rings, but not earrings? What was wrong with open-toed shoes? Why were her daughters not allowed to share clothing since they were the same size, and how did such sharing cause jealousy? Why was the assistant-pastor's wife allowed to wear the same dress that Bonnie had bought for her daughter but had had to return because it was "inappropriate"? Why was Carl allowed to break every one of his own child-rearing man- dates with his own grandchild? Why were the children not allowed to visit other churches, and why were families not allowed to visit relatives during the holidays? What was so wrong about missing *one* church service?

Bonnie began realizing that Carl's interpretation and practice of doctrine were not consistent with the Scriptures. There was an extreme emphasis on attitudinal sins such as rebelliousness and pride, and an unhealthy dependence among the congregation on their pastor. There was a total lack of accountability to any elders on Carl's part, a defensiveness of his ministry that grew over time, and a strong attitude of superiority and exclusivity. "No one else teaches the *whole* counsel of God like this." "Carl Plummer is our Apostle Paul."

Finally, shortly after Carl Plummer died, Keith and Bonnie Mason took their family out of Midvale Bible Church. The Masons have suffered much. Keith had written a secular song shortly before meeting Plummer. His pastor had told him to get rid of the "worldly" song, and Keith sold his rights for thirty-four dollars. To date, it has been recorded by three groups and has sold over three million copies. Fortunately, after a fifteen-year hiatus, Keith's music career is again on the rise.

Keith and Bonnie have been shunned by their former friends. Longtime associates of fifteen years turn their heads when they walk down the street. Bonnie says she does not care. She is glad to be free. She is, however, feeling very badly about her children. Both daughters became extremely rebellious when they moved away to college. They are doing things that she knows are wrong. Bonnie regrets not having had the opportunity to raise her children in a normal, healthy, Christian home, free of condemnation and the competition fostered by Plummer's teachings. She is jealous of others who have lived normal, Christian lives. She would like to regain the lost years.

Although Bonnie is not angry at God, she cannot yet forgive the Christians who have hurt her. The Plummer family has denied any wrongdoing and any manipulation or inappropriate actions on Carl's part. Bonnie blames them for the rebelliousness that her children are experiencing.

Bonnie knows that there is still much residual confusion and doubt to work through. She doesn't understand why God allowed the experiences of the past fifteen years. She is desperately looking for God to show her a way to go on with her life and to put the past behind her. As she says, she earnestly desires to "forget what is behind and strain toward what is ahead, to press on toward the goal to win the prize for which God has called me heavenward in Christ Jesus."

———————————◆———————————

Bonnie's story, as well as the other case histories presented in this book, points to the need on the part of Christians for discernment. At what point does biblical authority turn into spiritual violence? When does a church cross the line between conventional-church status and abusive-church status? What are some signals or indicators that a given group is headed for the margins?

It goes without saying that the pastoral leaders we have examined here are power-seeking individuals. In their attempts to control and manipulate others, they reveal much about their own personality and identity. Behavioral scientists view the desire for power as the result of a deep-seated insecurity or need. It is my impression that abusive pastors often come from troubled backgrounds and are very insecure persons despite the "take charge" image they may project. They are power-hungry people who crave visibility. Leaders who inflict spiritual violence often hide behind the smoke screen of authority to gain power.

However, as Cheryl Forbes correctly points out, the words *power* and *authority* are not synonymous.

Power means insistence on what we want for no other reason than that we want it; it means making other people follow us despite their own wishes. Power is assumed, insensitive, dehumanizing, and ultimately destructive. Authority, on the other hand, is positive, and usually involves a conferred right within strictly controlled bounds.[1]

Although she is not addressing specifically the topic of abusive churches, Forbes' analysis is directly applicable to the material I have presented in this book. Note this insightful observation:

The exercise of power always implies coercion and violence because the purpose of power is to reproduce itself. Whatever tries to prevent this reproduction must be disposed of. An exercise of authority, however, should have nothing to do with coercion, violence, or manipulation. Yet in our zeal for God's work we decide that if someone won't recognize our authority, we will force him with our power.[2]

Jesus is our ultimate role model when it comes to the exercise of power and authority. Even though unlimited power and authority in heaven and on earth were at his disposal, the Scripture clearly demonstrates that he was never on a power trip. "You know that the rulers of the Gentiles lord it over them," he once told his disciples, "and their high officials exercise authority over them. Not so with you. Instead, whoever wants to become great among you must be your servant, and whoever wants to be first must be your slave—just as the Son of Man did not come to be served, but to serve, and to give his life as a ransom for many" (Matt. 20:25-28).

John White and Ken Blue in their book, *Healing the Wounded*, address the problem of the spiritual tyranny that results when leaders abuse their authority and seek to subjugate Christians.

There is a tension among Christians that arises from what might be called a *high view of the church* and a *high view of Scripture*. Both have their dangers. The first emphasizes the authority of the church over the lives of God's people. Similarly a high view of Scripture emphasizes the need for Scripture to control the behavior of Christians. Both emphases are found in Scripture. There is no tension between them. The tension arises in the minds of leaders who try to use either church or Bible or both to control God's people. Church leaders are themselves under the authority of Scripture, but its authority is never to be coercive: it does not make leaders into rulers.[3]

Ruler is the right term to describe the kind of people in authoritarian leadership roles who are a focus of this book. They are spiritual tyrants who take unholy pleasure in requiring obedience and subordination of their followers. It is important to recognize that leadership depends on followership, and from a truly Christian perspective, that means cooperation *with* the leader rather than domination and control *by* the leader. The source of legitimate Christian leadership therefore lies in *entrusted authority.*

The spiritual autocrat, the religious dictator, attempts to *compel* subordination; the true Christian leader can legitimately only *elicit* followership.

Church leaders must be accountable both to God and to the congregations that they lead. They must strive to exemplify the qualities of our Lord Jesus Christ, "that great Shepherd of the sheep." "Leaders are meant to be facilitators not despots. Their role is essential. But they must use their authority in the way Jesus did. And they must never forget that while (like all of us) they have a line to heaven, unlike Jesus they are open to the wiles of the devil."[4]

It is common practice for pastors in abusive churches to fail to distinguish between spiritual and worldly authority. As John White and Ken Blue write:

> Occasionally, especially if they are young in age and inexperienced, they may say, "You must submit to me because God has placed me over you." Now while such words may be true, they are words that never fall from the lips of true leaders because the authority of true leaders springs from spiritual power. Such words prove the speaker's unfitness for his task. They too can enslave us to another gospel rather than draw us to the freedom of the cross.[5]

Pastor Phil Aguilar of Set Free Christian Fellowship likes to say, "It's my way or the highway." The arrogance of such a statement contrasts with the gentleness and humility of Christ's way. Pastor Don Barnett of Community Chapel communicated the same attitude: "I have the anointing and because I have the anointing, I know what I'm doing." That kind of thinking is obviously dangerous, but to many members of authoritarian churches it doesn't appear inappropriate. They look at their pastor and say, "How could a Spirit-filled, anointed pastor ever be wrong?" The young man whose case history follows found out the hard way what it means to be in the wrong church at the wrong time.

———————•◆•———————

Bruce Hogan says that he has been "recovering nicely" after six terrible years in the very militant Potter's House, also variously known as La Puerta (or, The Door), Victory Chapel, or Christian Fellowship Church, based in Prescott, Arizona. His involvement came about as the result of a spiritual quest he undertook after dropping out of high school. Having been brought up in what he terms a "traditional multidivorce family," with a father who left when he was three, Bruce says that he was searching for a real father. He has finally found his heavenly Father, but not before experiencing a great deal of pain and suffering at the hands of an abusive church. "I had no prior Christian experience or training and I didn't know how to spot a counterfeit. My home life was typical of the divorce and MTV generation, and I suppose I was looking for something like an artificial, ready-made family. Ignorance coupled with desire always results in trouble."

Bruce, now "twenty eight and looking like forty," had just left his job as a nightclub entertainer when he first encountered the Potter's House. He had found God on his eighteenth birthday while using "recreational chemical substances," and was "supernaturally saved" after years of delving into the occult, like his father before him. He believes that God did a real miracle to save him because the occult influence of his father had been passed down generationally.

Bruce, with no grounding in the Bible, had decided that he

had better quit his wild life-style and go to college. He had
passed the GED, and was just beginning Southeast Missouri
State University when members of the Potter's House first
arrived in town. Impressed by their zealousness, and
influenced by their concern, he joined their ranks in 1984.

Being a very intelligent and discerning person, Bruce was
concerned, even at the beginning of his involvement, about
the emphasis on authority, submission, and spiritual head-
ship. But he also thought that they might help him overcome
his terribly rebellious nature.

Bruce was self-supporting while at Southeast Missouri
State. Not only did he work full-time and take a full course
load, he also became involved in all the fellowship activities,
outreaches, revival meetings, and regular services of the
church. After a few months of little sleep and failing grades,
he landed in the hospital from sheer exhaustion. The
attending physician told him to stop the whirlwind of
activity or he would be dead in weeks.

However, with his salvation at stake, Bruce continued,
and, as he puts it, "sacrificed my higher critical thinking
faculties" to the leadership of the Potter's House. Week after
week of meetings and revivals that lasted late into the night
had done their job and caused him to "just stop thinking." "I
had surrendered the lordship over my life to a reprobate
mind" [that of the Potter's House leadership], and came to
recognize that "even the elect can be deceived."

Bruce believes that at its peak the Potter's House had a
network of hundreds of congregations. Committing very
little to paper, the leadership limits access to information to a
select few. Run by Wayland Mitchell out of Prescott,
Arizona, local congregations have no say as to who will lead
them. Bruce's local fellowship had three different pastors
during his stay, all of whom were sent from Prescott. He
describes the Potter's House movement as very aggressive,
strong on church planting, militantly committed, and very
anti-intellectual. He was called an "educated idiot with a
high IQ," and was told, "You obviously have a call on your
life, son. You should be pursuing ministry and submitting
yourself to our discipleship."

Bruce's inquisitive nature and analytical mind were always considered a manifestation of rebellion. When he attempted to show one of the elders that his teaching was not in line with the Scriptures, he was violently rebuked and told, "I am the shepherd. You are the sheep. God is my head covering, and I am answerable only to Him. And don't you forget it." Bruce says, "I wished John the Apostle were there. He'd be kicking some butt. . . . Pardon me. He would be setting things in theologically correct order."

It is Bruce's opinion that the Potter's House attracts those with altruistic natures who know little or nothing about God and the Scriptures but who are on a spiritual quest. It reaches "those strata and segments of society that no one else can touch." The problem is, Bruce says, that when people join, "they kill them," and if they ever leave the Potter's House, it is unlikely that they will ever serve the Lord again. The majority of the membership come to know God while in the fellowship—there is no Christian foundation outside of their Potter's House experience.

Bruce believes that his involvement in the Potter's House is his own fault. He has no excuse. "I had the Bible. I had the witness of the Holy Spirit. I knew something was wrong, but I thought it was just my own rebelliousness. . . . I fired the little lawyer inside me that tried to save me."

After six years of pastoral and psychological abuse, Bruce and his new wife left the Potter's House. He was "rescued" by George Orwell's *Animal Farm*, a book about totalitarianism that Bruce also feels accurately describes the Prescott-based fellowship. He admits that this was a unique aid to his exit, but reading the book sparked his abilities to think critically and independently.

The Potter's House, "first to condemn, first to judge, and last to show any mercy," shunned the Hogans. They were told that they were going to hell and that they had never been saved. They were also slandered by the leadership. "I was sacrificing babies in my basement or was a homosexual, or whatever." Eventually they left everything and moved away.

Having no church to go to that he felt he could trust, Bruce said, "The heck with it. I'm going to stay at home and read my Bible. 'Every man to his tent.'" Over six month's time, primarily because of being laid up from a severe, work-related back injury, Bruce came to know the truth in Scripture. Feeling very old now, he says, "God's people are destroyed for a lack of knowledge. I would have become a heretic if God had not put me on my back for six months. All I did was read the Bible."

Bruce, understandably, had difficulty with forgiveness. "In order to survive the ordeal of withdrawing from an authoritarian church, you have to admit that you have been taken and forgive from the heart. Otherwise, in the words of our Lord, you will be 'delivered to the tormentors.' When I finally forgave from my heart, I began to recover." His wit, though not as acerbic as a year ago, is still sharp. Paraphrasing Luther, he says, "If there be a hell, Prescott is built over it."

———————•◆•———————

As Bruce indicated, the membership of authoritarian churches is frequently comprised of young, spiritually immature Christians. This kind of church is successful because it is meeting basic human needs—the need to belong, the need to be affirmed, to be accepted, and to be part of a family. It is not unusual for the leaders to assume the role of surrogate parents, especially for those young adults who come from dysfunctional-family backgrounds. Speaking of the woman who was pastor of the Church of Jesus Christ Forever, a small, authoritarian congregation in the Midwest, one ex-member says this: "She really cared about us. We were young, looking for something, and she really took us under her wing." Echoing similar sentiments, a former member of an east coast group sums up the appeal of the abusive church she joined: "I never felt I had a family until I became part of this church. Never before had I felt so loved and cared for in every way. They were the first family I ever had."

Although they may be on the fringe of mainstream evangelicalism, spiritually abusive churches usually are closer to biblical orthodoxy than they are to outright heresy. Yet, there is often a subtle distortion of biblical teaching.

)erience at the Community of Jesus
member relates an all-too-common

be blinded, and you bend over
for your own good. . . . I think for me
le who were perhaps recently con-
have taken biblical truths, and the
but they are twisted, all twisted.
are of the twisting so that you accept it
:ause you see *them* [the leaders] as
that God's given us in the
say makes a good deal of sense. But
e application of it—and it's so subtle
ds—something in the way they apply
ng way.[6]

:ernment, then, is the recognition that
churches foster an unhealthy form of
ially and otherwise, by focusing on
themes of submission and obedience to those in authority.
They create the impression that people just aren't going to
find their way through life's maze without a lot of firm
directives from those at the top. They promote what MacDonald calls a form of "learned helplessness." He writes,
"Remarkably, many intelligent Christians actually enjoy
being told what to do. In GCI churches, people seek the
elders for permission to go home and see their parents or
friends, and to inquire for how long they may stay; they go to
them for permission to go to a party with unbelievers. . . ."[7]

The disquieting truth is that many Christians do indeed
fall into the trap of authoritarianism because of an inclination
toward the black-and-white mentality that abusive churches
cater to. If you have the type of personality that is drawn
toward groups that offer wraparound security and solutions
to all your problems, you are vulnerable to spiritual abuse. If
you value your spiritual autonomy, you must resist any
teaching that brings into question Christ's role as the sole
mediator (go-between) between God and humankind. No
Christian is ever called upon to give unquestioning obedience to anyone. Only Jesus Christ deserves disciples.

If you are a new convert, reaffirm the freedom that

characterizes the new life in Christ. Ironically, ex-members of Set Free Fellowship have an expression: "We've cut loose from Set Free." They found themselves in bondage rather than true freedom, subjected to spiritual infantilism and dependency rather than growth. However attractive and upbeat the group in question may at first appear to be, follow the example of the diligent Bereans who "examined the Scriptures every day to see if what Paul said was true" (Acts 17:11).

The discerning Christian must also beware of the trap of legalism. We have seen numerous examples throughout this book of how life-style rigidity and the keeping of a set of rules can stifle spiritual liberty and encourage abuse. Preoccupation with keeping Christian rules enhances guilt feelings in members, and it acts as an effective control mechanism for power abusers. "Legalism is never corrective church discipline. For legalism pulls us away from following Christ toward another gospel, another gospel that says the cross is not enough."[8]

Another quality that can lead to abusive behavior in a church is the tendency toward isolationism, a conscious effort to limit input from outside the church—in other words, information control. Beware of the church where outside speakers are consistently denied access to the pulpit, and where other Christian churches are regularly denounced, belittled, or ridiculed. Competing authority figures, whether from within or without the church walls, are rarely welcomed in abusive churches. No one can measure up to their exalted standards. In the words of Marie Kolasinski (see chapter 6), "Ninety-nine percent of the people who profess to be Christians are really enemies of the cross."

It is my opinion, based on extensive research and informal observation, that authoritarian leaders are ecclesiastical loners. That is, they do not function well or willingly in the context of systematic checks and balances. They are fiercely independent and refuse to be part of a structure of accountability. To put it crudely, they operate a one-man (or one-woman) spiritual show. And God help the person who gets in the way or makes waves. Yes, sometimes they will point to a board of elders or its equivalent, but more likely than not, this turns out to be a faithful inner circle of clones that implicitly accepts all that the leader sets forth.

As we have seen, another sign of impending trouble in a church is an obsession with discipline and excommunication. Beware of churches that warn of certain doom if you leave their "covering," or if you "break covenant." Once banished from the group, little compassion is shown the wayward one. An overwhelming majority of the ex-members I have interviewed expressed the opinion that abusive leaders are cold, almost cruel, in their treatment of people who leave—whether that departure was voluntary or involuntary. Almost without exception they report that the leadership made no attempt at reconciliation and made no effort to heal the wounds inflicted. Instead, defectors are held up to the congregation as warnings to potential "sowers of discord." As the leader of one small group in Delaware County, Pennsylvania, the Church of Our First Love, was quoted as saying, "Anyone who hinders the work I do, God will remove him."

Once he had decided to seek his spiritual food outside the Boston Movement, a former member of that group says he

> experienced the full force of friendly persuasion, peer pressure, righteous indignation, and eventually a form of "shunning," where one exists, but for all intents and purposes is "dead" in the eyes of the brothers and sisters. To leave the Boston Church of Christ—even to leave for another congregation of the Church of Christ—was not a recognized option; to leave was a weak, sinful thing to do, tantamount to opting for perdition.[9]

He adds, "Not once did I ever hear from a member of the Boston Church of Christ again."

A sure sign that a church is headed for the fringe is when family relationships are significantly disrupted and the leadership encourages the severing of ties with relatives outside of the group. "Be prepared to switch your loyalty from your natural family to God's family," advises Marie Kolasinski of the Body of Christ Fellowship. "Those blood ties are filthy rags unto God. So if you are experiencing great upheaval in your well-ordered natural family, BE OF GOOD

CHEER." When a Christian is asked to sacrifice family relationships for church loyalty, it's time to bail out.

In abusive-church situations, the "spiritual family" often displaces the biological family, and church leaders assume the role of surrogate parents. The founder of Great Commission International, Jim McCotter, is said to have usurped "the very authority of parents over these young people" by allowing youthful "elders" to exercise greater influence in the lives of the young adults than did their own parents.[10]

On the day after Mother's Day, 1991, two young members of Set Free Christian Fellowship, one of them the pastor's daughter-in-law, telephoned their Christian mothers to tell them they never wanted to see or hear from them again, in part because they (the mothers) had expressed their concerns about Set Free to newspaper reporters and to the author of this book. When one of those mothers and her husband later dropped off presents for grandchildren they were not permitted to visit, Pastor Phil Aguilar's son filed charges of trespassing with the local police—against his own in-laws. The gifts were returned to the grandparents in a large carton along with a note that read, "No thanks!"

When an evangelical church institutes a surveillance system and encourages its members to keep close tabs on one another, it's time to look for another church. A former member of the Boston Movement describes a scenario common to most abusive churches.

> Everyone's Christian life was under scrutiny by someone, assigned by some level of authority; each member was confronted with observed faults, issued counsel, and followed up; each was encouraged to know the true state of his own soul, its sins and weaknesses, and to confess these openly and honestly to others who have ministry and authority over him.[11]

The warning lights should register when a mainstream Christian church begins to show signs of an unhealthy elitism. This characteristic is related to the isolationist attitude I discussed earlier and is well illustrated by another example from the Boston Movement. A former member speaks of the Boston Church of Christ:

setting itself in bold, confrontational opposition to everyone not directly affiliated with itself. ... Access to this elite community is through the narrow gate of a baptism that is at once the product of an intensive "cost counting" process that results in a fully conscious subjection of one's entire self, as a repentant sinner, to Jesus' Lordship, a lifelong commitment to needs of the Body, and absolute obedience to the leaders of the movement.[12]

To the average Christian person reading this book, the examples of pastoral abuse and spiritual exploitation should represent a patent breach of biblical teaching. You may even feel that the abusive practices described in these pages appear to be far removed from the world of conventional churchgoers, and, it is hoped, they are.

Yet, I am convinced that tendencies toward abusive styles of leadership are more prevalent than most Christians realize. If we are honest with ourselves, we might admit that at least the *potential* for authoritarianism may exist in some of our own backyards.

I will discuss the problem and the challenge that this represents in the concluding chapter, but allow me to comment briefly here on a troublesome trend I see in the evangelical community today. It seems that we have a need to create evangelical gurus, Christian celebrities, super-pastors in megachurches, and miscellaneous other "teachers" and "experts" that *we* place on pastoral pedestals. What is it about people, including evangelicals, that explains this apparent need for authority figures, the need to have someone cosign for our lives? As David Gill noted years ago:

> We want heroes! We want reassurance that someone knows what is going on in this mad world. We want a father or a mother to lean on. We want revolutionary folk heroes who will tell us what to do until the rapture. We massage the egos of these demagogues and canonize their every opinion. We accept without a whimper their rationalizations of their errors and deviations.[13]

Christians, as well as other members of society, live in a culture that is rapidly changing and confusing. Many experience real insecurities and are attracted to organizations and churches that offer systematic approaches and clear-cut answers to life's problems. For people who come from dysfunctional families, or who have lacked structure in their lives, authoritarian churches are a haven, a womb of security. It is sometimes comforting to have others make decisions for you, tell you how to live, and tell you what to believe.

As James I. Packer reminds us in *Christianity Today*, the evangelical world is plagued by "the personality cult." We, the mainstream evangelical public, elevate certain individuals to virtual infallibility. "On issue after issue people reason thus: 'Billy Graham / Martyn Lloyd-Jones / John Wimber / John Stott / Chuck Swindoll / Elisabeth Elliot / R. C. Sproul / (write in here your own preferred authority) says it; I believe it; that settles it.'"[14]

In our homes, in our churches, and in our programs of Christian education, we must strive to cultivate critical, discerning minds if we are to avoid the tragedy of churches that abuse.

11

CHALLENGE AND CHANGE
ABUSIVE CHURCHES
WILL ALWAYS EXIST

11

CHALLENGE AND CHANGE
Abusive Churches
Will Always Exist

"We repented and were accepted back into fellowship, but they were afraid to associate with us again. When we came back, they didn't know what to say. They didn't know what was really wrong, what we'd done, or what they could say or shouldn't say that might make *them* fall from favor. They didn't know how to relate to us because I had been a 'leading brother' and had 'failed.' But, what really bothered me was, if our repentance was accepted and we were back, why didn't any other workers or leading brothers call to see how we were doing or drop by for tea or anything? They showed very little compassion."

Kyle Larson's story of his eleven-year involvement with George Geftakys' "Assembly" demonstrates every aspect of the psychological, emotional, and spiritual abuse that is characteristic of many fringe fundamentalistic churches. Kyle and his wife were "workers"—responsible under shepherds—in The Assembly's hierarchy of command. As such, they gave away eleven years of their lives, including their college careers, to follow "Brother George's" interpretation of the way to eternal life. Not once in their married life did they have any privacy, but lived with and spiritually directed as many as seventeen "brothers or sisters" at any given time.

The Assembly is based in Fullerton, California, where Brother George Geftakys, 64, a graduate of Talbot School of Theology and former Baptist minister, provides the model

for his followers across the country. Strongly influenced by
Plymouth Brethren thought and anti-denominational teaching that condemns organized Christianity, Brother George
began his ministry among the students of the hippie generation of the early 1970's. Drawing his following from Fullerton Junior College and California State University at Fullerton—"because the older people don't want to change and
are set in their ways"—Brother George began by speaking to
house meetings of loosely knit young Christians who had
come to Christianity out of the hippie movement. As Kyle
says, "We were willing to have anyone come speak to us who
wanted to address a group of Christians." None of these
young people knew much about the Bible or had any
developed discernment skills. All were "on fire for God,"
and desired a life-style of total commitment, including lives
as missionaries if that was God's will.

Brother George would speak to two southern California
communes called the House of Christian Love and the
House of the Lord's Grace on a regular basis. Kyle was
impressed. "He could really preach a sermon." On New
Year's weekend of 1971, Brother George invited his new
following to a seminar at Hillcrest Park in Fullerton. This
included members of the two communes as well as a few
young families who had been following him around to the
different Bible studies where he would teach. At that time,
Kyle and his contemporaries had been Christian believers
for about six months. "He began opening the Scriptures to us
and showing us what it meant to be involved in a corporate
testimony." By February of that year the thirty-five persons
in attendance began to meet regularly under George's
teaching. The recreation center of Hillcrest Park had been
offered by the city to the fledgling church free of charge on
Sundays in hopes that they would be a positive influence on
a bad neighborhood.

Kyle recalls that within six months a leadership board
composed of "leading brothers" had been chosen by Brother
George. The initial authority exercised by George seemed to
be good. Brothers and sisters were separated into different
houses located in the area, and a strict regimen of activities
was begun. This was all completely opposite to the laid-back

life-style to which the members had been accustomed. The Christian communes of the earlier period had been very loosely structured. "We didn't have rules or regulations; we came and went as we pleased. We just lived together because to us, it was a very normal outgrowth of the kind of life-style we had had before."

The new "brothers' houses" were very regimented with nightly meetings, shared expenses, and shared tasks around the house. (Similar "sisters' houses" came into being a few years later.) Everyone was expected and required to attend all meetings, and there were at least six of them each week. All of this was in addition to being full-time students. Consequently, many never finished college.

Kyle says that "George has a very domineering personality and is extremely opinionated and dogmatic. He has a way of looking at the world that's not quite real, and he's also extremely intelligent." Although he always refers to himself as a "brother among brothers," there is no question in anyone's mind who is in charge of The Assembly. As Kyle states, "It was clear, without a doubt, who the leader was, who was giving the direction, the counsel, the teaching. It was George. That position, from the very beginning, was secured. I don't think that it was ever relinquished for even a moment."

Brother George asserts that he runs a "prophetic ministry." He teaches a great deal on how believers are to relate to him as "The Lord's Servant" who has been anointed by God. While he never refers to himself as *the* servant of the Lord, and does not claim to have a unique anointing himself, he doesn't have to. For his followers there is an implicit understanding that Brother George is "the Lord's Servant" in the ministry to whom all are subject and to whom each is loyal.

The group's name, "The Assembly," came about as a reaction against the organized church. It was said that the word "church" had a bad connotation. "Church is a building and it's used wrongly. We are the Assembly; we are the *ecclesia* [the 'called out ones'—the assembly of God's people]; we take no name other than Christ—no name, just 'The Assembly'." Their anti-denominational stance has gotten them confused with Witness Lee's "Local Church" at times, and, as Kyle indicates, they have had some "very big clashes" with members of the "Local Church" movement. Both groups disdain organized Christianity (reflecting Plymouth Brethren influences on both), but The Assembly does not engage in "pray reading" and other practices associated with the "Local Church" movement.

Kyle and his wife were known as "workers." Workers were the ones most closely associated with Brother George and constituted his "inner group." A list of twenty-eight characteristics was developed to describe the requirements for workers. Set within these guidelines is the key notion that, in effect, Brother George is "The Lord's Servant" to whom everyone must be subject and to whom everyone must be loyal. The inner core of workers oversees the whole ministry of The Assembly, while each local Assembly is directed by a leading brothers' council.

Kyle states that during the early years, "Brother George spoke on Sunday morning, Brother George spoke on Sunday afternoon, and Brother George spoke on Wednesday night. Brother George spoke at the prayer meetings, and he spoke on Saturday morning." He spent those first years indoctrinating the workers into "all his thoughts, his ideas, everything, until the brothers were 'developed.'" Thereafter, some of the more "mature" brothers were allowed to "get a word" and preach. However, no one from the outside was ever allowed to address The Assembly. Brother George's followers regarded him like the apostle Paul, his role being to plant Assemblies, preach, and give the vision.

Kyle now realizes that much of what he and the other members did was a direct result of what George said they could do—or had to do. "Although we were getting older and were no longer kids anymore, we were still treated very much in that same manner." Those who fell from favor with George, particularly the older members who persisted in questioning his teaching and authority, were ostracized and ridiculed. "You don't have a relationship with George unless George dominates."

Brother George would save his most extreme indoctrination for the workers' meetings—because workers were supposed to develop "thick skins." Although he reserved much of the verbal and psychological abuse for private sessions, he would ridicule dissenters in these closed workers' meetings, gatherings to which the general congregation was neither invited nor allowed to attend.

The average members, according to Kyle, don't see the underside of the organization. "They see the enthusiasm, the tremendous amount of outreach that goes on, the impressive amount of personal involvement, and the companionship as you labor together with them." But they were not privy to the inner details of "The Work"—leading, discipling, decision-making, problem solving, and indoctrinating. The written code of requirements for workers states that, "The Work is not conducted on the basis of democracy. . . . We have the right to demand loyalty in The Work. . . . We come into The Work. . .with a commitment to The Work. . . ."

Supposedly, any Christian is welcome to attend meetings at The Assembly, and to partake of the Lord's Supper with them. No one is turned away, and, "God's family and God's purpose are inclusive of everyone." However, former members say the principle is not carried out in practice.

Kyle and his wife had a difficult time leaving The Assembly because to leave was to lose one's "covering." To leave would be to subject oneself to physical danger from the Adversary, or to the defilement of one's testimony by Satan. Members are continually taught that "there is no place else in the world like this Assembly in Fullerton." Kyle says that the spiritual intimidation employed can be severe. Members are brought before the leading brothers' council and "talked to" for violations such as displaying a desire to hear other Christian preachers, having a "rebellious spirit," disagreeing with authority, lack of subjection to the leadership, questioning one of Brother George's teachings, or desiring to go to another church. "You have one person on one side of the table, with an array of men on the other side. A domineering person is telling you you're wrong, why you're wrong, that you need to repent, and then, one by one, all the rest of them agree wholeheartedly. The targeted person has a tremendous psychological onslaught to deal with. More often than not, he ends up in tears and repents, and is either eventually restored to favor or leaves the fellowship." Additionally, peer pressure among the general congregation is an extremely effective tool used to control the wayward.

Although members are taught that it is perfectly legitimate to have differences of opinion between "godly men," in practice it is not allowed. Brother George himself claims to be accountable to the leading brothers, and that he doesn't do anything without their approval. However, "they always agree with him," because, "Brother George has insight to see things that we don't see." As a result, Brother George and a few of his underlings exercise unrestrained control in the lives of Assembly members. Followers are told what occupations are God-honoring, whether or not they may practice the professions for which they have been trained, whom they can marry and when, where they can live, whom they can date, what they can do with their money, and, in some instances, what they can and cannot eat.

Members of The Assembly are in a real double bind when it comes to family and children. Although there is a great emphasis on homes and the need for family life, activities are so frequent and so intense that children are neglected. Families are lucky to have two Saturdays a year to spend together, Kyle observes. From birth children are expected to attend all meetings and to remain quiet "in the presence of the Lord." "You would feel guilty if you went off with your family or just wanted to hang out. If you took off on a holiday to visit other family members, you just didn't want what the Lord wanted, and you were just going the way of the world."

The requirements on workers are the most intense and burdensome, often entailing voluminous correspondence, outreach efforts, and meetings. And, of course, Sunday is reserved entirely as a day for the Lord.

Brother George teaches in "broad strokes"—a whole chapter from the Bible at a time. He may use three- or four-hundred Scriptures in a two-hour meeting, and in the midst of all the Scriptures he is attempting to identify a general pattern or teaching. He tells his followers that he believes that the vast majority will "forsake him in the end," but that if only one or two remain loyal it will have been worth his effort. In the end, "tremendous persecution" will inevitably be his lot. Members are encouraged not to miss out, but to overcome and receive their "inheritance."

Brother George believes that the greatest part of salvation is yet to come. According to his theology, only overcomers— those in The Assembly—will reign with Christ in the millennial kingdom, which is their inheritance for appropriating God's grace. At the end of the millennium and after the destruction of Satan, all believers will gain entrance to the eternal kingdom, but only those having an inheritance will reign first.

In order to maintain full control over the lives of his followers, Brother George instituted a reporting system by which he rewards those who inform him of any questionable activities among the membership. Although "everyone would deny that flatly," it was understood that those who informed on others were "truly godly," and that the "dedicated ones told all." Consequently, Kyle, and many others, confided in no one, including even their spouses at times. Special friendships were said to cloud one's ability to really discern the Lord. Affections might get in the way of making an objective spiritual judgment or decision concerning someone in The Work.

Brother George has developed a teaching that refutes all criticism. He encourages members to listen to no criticism of or accusations against that teaching whatsoever, even "the Enemy" lurking in one's own thoughts. The result of this teaching, according to Kyle, is the "subtle cutting off of any kind of critical thinking, any kind of analytical thinking." Members therefore listen to nothing but the teachings of Brother George.

Kyle and his wife believe that they remained with The Assembly as long as they did because they were away from Fullerton and the full impact of George's influence for six of their eleven years. During that time they ministered to Assemblies in several states. Kyle says, "When we started thinking that we were going to be coming back to Fullerton, we very seriously considered not even leaving the Midwest, just because we had personally been out from under all the control for so long. It was a lot easier to deal with a long-distance phone call than it was to deal with discipline day-by-day, face-to-face. When we were told to move to another city, we thought that that was a little bit better. But, what it comes down to is that there are always ways for control to be established and perpetuated no matter where you are. The appropriate thing to say to Brother George was always, 'Brother, whatever you want me to do, I'll do it.'"

Eventually, Kyle "fell into sin" and was excommunicated. In actuality, he left the movement for a period of time because he was "fed up." He had begun to see the subtle indoctrination process involving heavy scheduling, constant teaching, unending meetings, and the partisan viewpoint being presented while passed off as inspiration from God. He saw the "tremendous psychological chains" that were being put on the people, and he was also aware that most people who leave The Assembly drift away from the Lord. They give up, believing that God himself has laid on them unachievable expectations.

Unable to reconcile his thoughts and sort out his emotions, Kyle "repented" and went through a yearlong process of proving his repentance to the leading brothers. He was passed up for four months during communion, and the condition of his repentance was based on how willing he was to do whatever he was told. Even when his repentance was accepted, he and his wife were still shunned, because members were afraid of associating with a fallen worker. After six months of this treatment, Kyle and his wife left to begin a new life.

———————————◆———————————

Leaders who are abusive usually develop their heavy-handed style over a period of time. Churches that abuse are the result of an ever-accelerating emphasis on the kinds of control mechanisms I have discussed in this book. People who have been in close contact over a period of years with some of the pastoral leaders we have discussed have told me that their ministry was far more benign and subdued at the beginning. Gradually, as the pastors became aware of the influence they could exert and the power they could wield, they and their ministries began to change. Consciously or unconsciously, they took advantage of vulnerable people, and convinced them that God had given them, the shepherds, the right to exercise authority over the flock.

> People who abuse power are changed progressively as they do so. In abusing power they give themselves over to evil, untruth, self-blindness, and hardness without allowing themselves or anyone else to see what is happening. The longer the process continues, the harder repentance becomes. Church bosses must be spotted and rescued early, or they may never be rescued at all. They have caused inconceivable havoc among churches throughout history.[1]

Pastoral abuse can be spotted quite easily, at least in its advanced stages. Abusive religion substitutes human power for true freedom in Christ. Unquestioning obedience and blind loyalty are its hallmarks. Leaders who practice spiritual abuse exceed the bounds of legitimate authority and "lord it over the flock," often intruding into the personal lives of members. God's will is something that *they* determine for you rather than something you individually seek to know. Abusive leaders are self-centered and adversarial rather than reconciling and restorative.

But what about rescuing the leaders and salvaging the followers? That is a major challenge facing the conventional evangelical church. Most of the abusive churches I have studied are independent, autonomous groups. They are not a part of a denomination or network that could provide checks and balances or any kind of accountability. As we have seen over and over again in these pages, their leaders are accountable to no one and resist any outside scrutiny. How can such independent groups *themselves* be disciplined or even investigated for aberrations? Because we value freedom of religion for all people and because we are reluctant to get involved in someone else's vineyard, even if we know it is "off the wall," the problem of abusive churches is likely to continue.

The key to understanding the whole phenomenon is within the human psyche—the desire to control others and to exercise power over people. That has always been a part of the human experience and it will continue to be. All of us have been exposed to the temptation of power, whether as parent, spouse, teacher, or worker. It has been said that human nature is always ready to abuse its power the moment it can do so with impunity. It should not be surprising, then, that the will to power sometimes invades the religious realm, and specifically the church.

The respected Christian writer and physician, Paul Tournier, writes that "there is in us, especially in those whose intentions are of the purest, an excessive and destructive will to power which eludes even the most sincere and honest self-examination."[2] He makes the point that people in the helping professions—social workers, physicians, psychologists, and pastors—especially need to be aware of the temptation of power, the temptation to manipulate, and to control those who come seeking help. "To be looked upon as a savior leaves none of us indifferent."

Although he was not specifically addressing the problem of contemporary pastoral abuse, Tournier's comments about the possibility of misusing spiritual authority are a timely warning.

> They look upon us as experts, God's mouthpieces, the interpreters of his will—to begin with for ourselves, but very soon, before we realize it, for other people too, especially since they insist on requiring it of us. Very soon, too, we find ourselves thinking that when they follow our advice they are obeying God, and that when they resist us they are really resisting God.[3]

While we probably cannot prevent individual power-seekers from getting entangled in their own authoritarian excesses, we must remind all who will hear, including mainstream Christian leaders, that weakness and dependence on God's strength are the hallmarks of true greatness. As Harold Bussell writes in *Unholy Devotion*:

> The antithesis of the misuse of power is gentleness, which is best seen and understood within the framework of strength. Gentle leaders, pastors, or teachers do not force their insights and wisdom on the unlearned, nor flaunt their gifts before those in need. They are patient. They take time for those who are slow to understand. They are compassionate with the

weak, and they share with those in need. Being a gentle pastor, shepherd, leader, or teacher is never a sign of being weak, but of possessing power clothed in compassion.[4]

This is in stark contrast to the style of abusive leaders, who, as we have seen, often lack compassion and a gentle spirit. Power has a way of blinding the conscience so that those who spiritually and psychologically abuse others (like abusive parents) show little sign of remorse and repentance. They deny any guilt for what they have done to people. And they project their own weaknesses onto others.

If we are in positions of power over others and we fail to place controls on ourselves, we subtly and unknowingly start to control others. Power that elevates a leader beyond contradiction . . .will lead both the leader and the followers down a road marked by broken relationships, exploitation, and control. Power that tempers and checks itself and is wrapped in compassion is the pathway to gentleness, caring, and maturity. Jesus said, "I am the good shepherd. The good shepherd lays down his life for the sheep" (John 10:11). He is our model of service and leadership.[5]

One of the pressing needs of the Christian church is to assist in the development of discernment skills among believers so that the likelihood of following an aberrant teacher or a false doctrine is diminished. The need for discernment was impressed on me by a former member of Hobart Freeman's Faith Assembly. He told me how the emphasis on the "faith message" or "faith walk" eventually diverted his focus from the centrality of Jesus Christ.

"The faith message is a counterfeit, unbiblical faith," he said. "It takes the place of relationship with Jesus. Christ became a secondary figure. We were taught that if you produce the works of faith, God will bless you and you will have definite proof that you are following Jesus Christ. These people would say, 'I believe with all my heart that I'm on the right track because Jesus healed me. Jesus gave me a promotion. Jesus gave me a new car. He gave me the desires of my heart.' It becomes a matter of the work of faith, doing some kind of faith formula. What *you* do is important proof of your salvation, not what *Jesus* did for your salvation."

This young man described the appeal of emphasizing positive thinking or "positive confession," as it is known in the faith movement. Many new Christians that he knew in the movement were not only attracted to Hobart Freeman, but to the prospect of supernatural, extraordinary experiences. "People look for teachers who claim special revelations, who promise signs and wonders. They've got to have something more than just a relationship with Jesus Christ."

One survivor of an abusive-church situation told me how she had been exposed to "every movement or fad that has crossed America in the past decade." Initially influenced by John Wimber's "signs and wonders" teachings, her church moved from an emphasis on healing to inner healing, visualization, the healing of memories, deliverance, positive confession, covenant relationships, prosperity teaching, discipling/shepherding, and even community living. She left confused and suffering from spiritual burn-out. "It's still difficult for me to read my old Bible, you know, the 'cool' one that's all marked up. I have to read a different translation. I can't sing the same worship songs and I have difficulty going to church."

This woman's comments about the progression of spiritual fads she encountered brings to mind a book that has not received wide circulation, but which I believe deserves thoughtful consideration by every Christian interested in the topic of current evangelical/charismatic movements. It is entitled *Wonders and the Word,* and is a collection of essays that sensitively and discerningly critique the Vineyard movement founded and headed by John Wimber. (There are now more than two hundred Vineyard fellowships throughout North America and Vineyard-sponsored seminars are held throughout Europe, the United Kingdom, South Africa, Australia, and New Zealand.) Although the book focuses on the "signs and wonders" emphasis within the Vineyard fellowship, I feel its message has wider implications for understanding any new religious movement.

I receive many inquiries about the Vineyard movement. Based on extensive conversations with both current and former members of Wimber's fellowship, I believe that the issues raised in *Wonders and the Word* are valid concerns and that this rapidly growing movement has great *potential* for problems similar to those I have been discussing in this book. Indeed, there is some evidence of abusive practices already taking place within Vineyard churches.

Let it be clearly understood that I agree with one of the contributors to *Wonders and the Word* when he states that

the Vineyard movement is impacting many people both inside and outside the church. We cannot deny its existence as a genuine work of the Spirit, and so should not discredit it. . . . At the same time, we need to be aware of some of the extremes to which such a movement can go. . . . Most new movements of the Holy Spirit are embraced by eager followers, many of whom tend to push the ideas of the leaders to extremes. However, rather than write off the movement because of excesses, we should draw alongside to render guidance and counsel where it is needed and welcomed.[6]

It is precisely this need and desire to provide counsel and guidance that constitutes the challenge to the larger Christian community as we reflect on the problem of abusive churches and the prospect of *potentially* abusive groups. As I shall point out shortly, there are some groups that are open to dialogue with more mainstream churches. Others are extremely defensive and resist any overtures from traditional churches, considering them to be apostate and outside the circle of the elect.

Another challenge to the larger Christian world includes the recognition that at least some of the members of abusive groups are refugees from more conventional evangelical churches. They are sincere, earnest seekers after God who, for a variety of reasons, have become disillusioned with mainstream evangelicalism. Many are seeking an intimacy and a kind of fellowship that traditional churches often do not provide. As Yeakley admits, "In the modern church, people come together as strangers and leave as strangers and their lives never touch."[7]

Others seek a more informal, charismatic worship style that many traditional evangelical churches do not offer. Interestingly, it is this dimension—worship style—that former members of abusive churches tell me they miss the most, as they reflect back on their experience. Still others mention the appeal of a familylike environment. I have in my files a letter from a man whose comment is not at all unusual: "One of the good things about the group was that it gave people like me a sense of 'family' and 'belonging' to an extent that I haven't had before or since."

Why are Christians being attracted to nontraditional groups? In addition to the reasons just cited—greater freedom in worship, acceptance, fellowship, and a sense of family—there is the appeal and excitement of experience, the desire for something new, something more, as illustrated by this observation concerning the Vineyard: "Dissatisfaction with a lack of spiritual power, a feeling of unfulfillment in one's relationship to Christ and a hunger for a new and deeper experience with God. . . . The Vineyard's emphasis on power, signs and wonders has a definite appeal to those who are searching for something more."[8]

I have already noted the role of subjective experience in the devolution of many abusive churches. It is understandable, then, that I voice my concern over the current preoccupation in some Christian circles, including the Vineyard movement, with the exorcism of demons, the pronouncements of "prophets" like Paul Cain and Bob Jones, the talk of a "new breed" of people ("Joel's Army"—a unique end-time army of believers endowed with supernatural power enabling them to perform "signs and wonders," purify the church, and overcome all opposition to the Gospel), the appearance of the "Manifest Sons of God," the unorthodox God-man theology of Benny Hinn, and the "revelation teaching" of assorted "end-time prophets" in charismatic circles. Space does not permit discussion of these phenomena, but let the reader beware.

As Dr. Paul G. Hiebert of Trinity Evangelical Divinity School correctly observes:

> Like most movements in the church, the current emphasis on healing, prophecy and exorcism has both positive and negative sides to it. It reminds us of the need to take seriously the work of the Holy Spirit in meeting everyday human needs. It is in danger, however, of placing primary emphasis on what is of secondary importance in scripture and of bending the

gospel to fit the spirit of our times. Satan often tempts us at the point of our greatest strengths. His method is not to sell us rank heresy, but to take the good we have and distort it by appealing to our self-interests.[9]

Abusive churches are not, for the most part, promoting rank heresy. But their human leaders seem ever willing to make pronouncements in the name of God, thus "mistaking what God is saying in Scripture for their own particular brand of interpretation of Scripture."[10] This sets the stage for the possibility of outright heresy being introduced, as well as the kind of abusive practices we have discussed.

Is it possible for authoritarian churches to change direction? There are several fairly recent examples of leaders who have announced changes and confessed to error. One of the leaders of the discipleship/shepherding movement officially known as Christian Growth Ministries, Bob Mumford, made a dramatic about-face after issuing a public statement of repentance in November of 1989. Mumford, one of the "Ft. Lauderdale Five" (so named because of the group of the five founders of Christian Growth Ministries of Ft. Lauderdale— Don Basham, Ern Baxter, Bob Mumford, Derek Prince, and Charles Simpson), acknowledged abuses that had occurred because of his teaching on submission. This emphasis resulted in "perverse and unbiblical obedience" to leaders. He publicly repented "with sorrow" and asked for forgiveness. He also admitted that families had been severely disrupted and lives turned upside down.

In an interview with *Christianity Today* magazine, Mumford indicated that the abuse of spiritual authority led to "injury, hurt, and in some cases, disaster." Leaders, he said, were operating at a level where biblical limitations on their authority were not clear. "Part of the motivation behind my public apology is the realization that this wrong attitude is still present in hundreds of independent church groups who are answerable to no one."[11]

Jack Hayford, whose counseling of Mumford was instrumental in the decision to issue a public apology, said in *Ministries Today* magazine that he was one of hundreds of pastors who had spent fifteen years "picking up the pieces of broken lives that resulted from distortion of truth by extreme teachings and destructive applications on discipleship, authority, and shepherding."[12]

In November of 1989, Maranatha Christian Churches, founded by Bob Weiner, announced that it was disbanding and dissolving its international federation of churches. The youth and inexperience of its pastors, along with the controversial shepherding practices of the group were some of the problems that led to the demise of the organization (although MCM spokespersons denied those allegations). Most of the churches themselves did not close, but instead became even more independent and autonomous bodies.

One of the most encouraging evidences of change appears to be taking place within the Great Commission Association of Churches, formerly named Great Commission International (GCI). Founder Jim McCotter is no longer associated with the organization. The current leadership (which includes many of the original leaders) has been consulting with evangelical pastors, lay persons, former members, and various well-known Christian organizations in an effort to chart a new course. I have met with several of the national leaders on two occasions, and I am convinced of their sincerity in wanting to begin a process of restoration and healing, as well as their desire to chart an organizational change.

The Great Commission leadership has sought to identify a number of "errors and weaknesses" that they feel were caused by incorrect or imbalanced teaching, the youthful immaturity of some leaders, and a number of other factors. In personal correspondence with me, one of their national leaders stated, "We have a desire to forthrightly acknowledge errors and problems that existed and yet not inaccurately or needlessly dishonor what the Lord has done in our past. . . ."

Former members of GCI are cautiously optimistic about the unfolding events and, frankly, they are a bit surprised. Others are more cynical, fearing that the effort is an insincere gesture in order to achieve acceptance and legitimation from the evangelical mainstream without fully acknowledging the depths of the hurt which has been caused over the years. At this writing, the effort at reconciliation and restoration is in process. Many will be watching to see the outcome and the nature of change that emerges. The Great Commission Association of Churches may well prove to be a model for other authoritarian groups to emulate.

Major change is also taking place within a network of charismatic Catholic communities because of the efforts of former members to expose the excessive control and abusive practices alleged to have occurred. The Word of God Community in Ann Arbor, Michigan, has undergone a split, and cofounders Ralph Martin and Steve Clark have experienced a parting of the ways. Word of God leaders, in a March 1991 letter to members, expressed a desire to repent of "spiritual pride and arrogance, elitism, legalism and an overbearing exercise of pastoral authority." Several months later the same leaders told assembled members that people were no longer to be under anyone's control, in effect renouncing the shepherding practices of the past. The basic issue that divides Martin and Clark is the nature of pastoral care and authority in Christian community. Martin's faction has opted for a more moderate pastoral system with less emphasis on submission, while Clark maintains that covenant community leaders have been entrusted with the spiritual and material welfare of the members, and therefore must exercise responsible pastoral authority over those members.[13]

Former members of several other charismatic Catholic communities told the *National Catholic Reporter* stories of the extreme submission of women to men, and life-style conformity that included the wearing of shoes and hairstyles similar to those of the leaders. One group celebrated the birth of boys but reportedly only "tolerated" newborn girls. A former member of one group was "discouraged" from visiting his dying mother. "He was told to repent for spending a Sunday morning with her."[14]

Roman Catholic Bishop Albert Ottenweller of Steubenville, Ohio, ordered an investigation of Servants of Christ the King, a charismatic covenant community affiliated with the Sword of the Spirit, a network of communities scattered throughout the United States and abroad. Bishop Ottenweller criticized the Servants of Christ the King for "an arrogance that is elitist. . ." and a "lack of compassion and love for those in need." He charged that the lives of members had been controlled through the manipulation of marriages and life-style patterns. "Great psychological harm has been done to members."[15]

While not all groups affiliated with the Sword of the Spirit have recanted their clearly abusive methods, the actions of Word of God leaders in Ann Arbor appear to be sincere and will have an uncertain but dramatic impact on that organization's future. In an interview with *Fidelity*, a conservative Catholic magazine, Word of God senior head-coordinator Ralph Martin admitted that the community had had problems from its earliest days.

> I think a small group of people basically took control of the whole thing early on. And I was part of that group. . . . I think [we] took the place of the Lord Himself, in a certain kind of way. Instead of trusting in the Lord and being docile to the Lord, . . .[we] basically got into protecting our thing, our work, in a way which led to excessive exercises of authority, controlling people's lives.[16]

While these examples of repentance and change are welcomed and praiseworthy, we must not forget those whose lives have been damaged, some irreparably, during the long years when the now-repentant leaders were unresponsive to warnings and reluctant to admit weakness. It is easy for us who have not experienced the pain and turmoil of their followers to say, "Forgive and forget."

We all struggle on in a fallen world, seeking to test the voices that call to us, to discern whether they are, indeed, from God. The ultimate challenge is to fix our eyes on Jesus, the Great Shepherd, who knows his sheep and who will never abandon us.

———————•◆•·•———————

> The word of the LORD came to me: "Son of man, prophesy against the shepherds of Israel. . . 'This is what the Sovereign LORD says: Woe to the shepherds of Israel who only take care of themselves! Should not shepherds take care of the flock? . . . . You have not strengthened the weak or healed the

sick or bound up the injured. You have not brought back the strays or searched for the lost. You have ruled them harshly and brutally. So they were scattered because there was no shepherd. . . . Therefore, you shepherds, hear the word of the LORD. . .because my shepherds did not search for my flock but cared for themselves rather than for my flock. . . . I am against the shepherds and will hold them accountable for my flock. I will remove them from tending the flock. . . . I myself will search for my sheep and look after them. . . . I will bind up the injured and strengthen the weak. . . . I will shepherd the flock with justice. . . . I will save my flock, and they will no longer be plundered. . . . You my sheep, the sheep of my pasture, are people, and I am your God, declares the Sovereign LORD.' " (Excerpts from Ezekiel 34)

Notes

Chapter 1

[1]Robert Coles, *Migrants, Sharecroppers, Mountaineers* (Boston: Little, Brown and Company, 1971), 41.
[2]Ibid., 42.

Chapter 3

[1]Martin E. Marty, *Pilgrims in Their Own Land* (New York: Penguin, 1984), 341.
[2]Ibid., 349.
[3]Shirley Nelson, *Fair Clear and Terrible* (Latham, N.Y.: British American Publishing, 1989), 57.
[4]Ibid., 67.
[5]Ibid., 381.
[6]Ibid., 191.
[7]Ibid., 162.
[8]Ibid., 248–49.
[9]Ibid., 133.
[10]Ibid., 127.
[11]Ibid., 148.
[12]Ibid., 205.
[13]Ibid., 253.
[14]Ibid., 105–06.
[15]Ibid., 106.
[16]Ibid., 90.
[17]Ibid., 252.
[18]Ibid., 91.
[19]Ibid., 218.
[20]Ibid., 254.
[21]Ibid., 160.
[22]Ibid., 224.
[23]Ibid., 165.
[24]Ibid., 208.
[25]Ibid., 209.
[26]Ibid., 210.

[27]Ibid., 236–37.
[28]Ibid., 329.
[29]Ibid., 431.

Chapter 5

[1]Jerry P. MacDonald, " 'Reject the Wicked Man': Coercive Persuasion and Deviance Production: A Study of Conflict Management," *Cultic Studies Journal,* vol. 5, No. 1, 1988, 59–121.
[2]Flavil Yeakley, *The Discipling Dilemma* (Nashville: Gospel Advocate, 1988), 33.
[3]Ibid., 34, 35, 37, 47.
[4]MacDonald, "Reject the Wicked Man," 75.

Chapter 6

[1]Jerry Jones, *What Does the Boston Movement Teach?* Vol. 1 (Bridgeton, MO: Mid-America Book and Tape Sales, 1990), 7–8.
[2]Ibid., 12.
[3]Jerry Jones, *What Does the Boston Movement Teach?* Vol. 2 (Bridgeton, MO: Mid-America Book and Tape Sales, 1990), 17.
[4]Ibid., 14.
[5]Flavil Yeakley, *The Discipling Dilemma* (Nashville: Gospel Advocate, 1988), 54–55.
[6]Melinda Keller, "Piecemakers: Kolasinski's Path to God," *Costa Mesa News* (August 5, 1988).
[7]Ibid.
[8]Melinda Keller, "Piecemakers: The Crafting of a Cult," *Costa Mesa News* (July 22, 1988).
[9]Ibid.
[10]Melinda Keller, "Piecemakers: Life in the Family of God," *Costa Mesa News* (August 19, 1988).

Chapter 7

[1]Russell Chandler, "Nameless Sect Travels 'Secret Path,'" *Los Angeles Times* (September 13, 1983), Part I: 1, 3, 17.
[2]"Abuse in the Truth," Spokane: Threshing Floor Ministries n.d., 2–3.
[3]Chandler, "Nameless Sect Travels 'Secret Path,'" 3.
[4]"Abuse in the Truth," 3.
[5]See chapter six of my book, *The Lure of the Cults and New Religions* (Downers Grove: InterVarsity, 1983).

Chapter 8

[1]"Abuse in the Truth," Spokane: Threshing Floor Ministries, n.d., 2.

[2]MacDonald, " 'Reject the Wicked Man': Coercive Persuasion and Deviance Production: A Study of Conflict Management," *Cultic Studies Journal,* Vol. 5, No.1, (1988), 48.

[3]Ibid., 88–89.

[4]Ibid., 82.

[5]*The Cape Codder,* April 19, 1985.

Chapter 9

[1]Greg O'Brien, "Ex-Community Members Deal With Fear and Guilt, Two Counselors Say," *The Cape Codder* (April 19, 1985).

[2]Jerry P. MacDonald, "Manipulation of the Scriptures Within Great Commission International," unpublished paper (1985), 186.

[3]Ibid.

[4]Ibid., 187.

Chapter 10

[1]Cheryl Forbes, *The Religion of Power* (Grand Rapids: Zondervan, 1983), 87.

[2]Ibid., 88.

[3]John White and Ken Blue, *Healing the Wounded: The Costly Love of Church Discipline* (Downers Grove, Ill.: InterVarsity, 1985), 39–40.

[4]Ibid., 41.

[5]Ibid., 84.

[6]Greg O'Brien and Paul Kemprecos, "Defectors Raise Questions About Religious Group," *The Cape Codder* (April 19, 1985).

[7]MacDonald, "Manipulation of the Scriptures," unpublished paper (1985), 192.

[8]White and Blue, *Healing the Wounded,* 83.

[9]Jones, *The Boston Movement,* vol. 2, 78.

[10]MacDonald, "Manipulation of the Scriptures," 153.

[11]Jones, *The Boston Movement,* vol. 2, 84.

[12]Ibid., 87.

[13]Quoted in Ronald M. Enroth, "The Power Abusers," *Eternity* (October, 1979), 25.

[14]James I. Packer, "How Will I Be Remembered?" *Christianity Today* (June 24, 1991), 11.

Chapter 11

[1]White and Blue, *Healing the Wounded* (Downers Grove, Ill.: InterVarsity, 1985), 198.

[2]Paul Tournier, *The Violence Within* (San Francisco: Harper & Row, 1978), 137.

[3]Ibid., 148.

[4]Harold Bussell, *Unholy Devotion* (Grand Rapids: Zondervan, 1983), 70.

[5]Ibid., 72.

[6]John Schmidt, "New Wine from the Vineyard," in *Wonders and the Word*, ed. James R. Coggins and Paul G. Hiebert (Hillsboro, Kansas: Kindred Press, 1989), 78–79.

[7]Flavil Yeakley, *The Discipling Dilemma* (Nashville: Gospel Advocate, 1988), 79.

[8]*Wonders and the Word*, 79.

[9]Paul G. Hiebert, "Healing and the Kingdom," in *Wonders and the Word*, ed. Coggins and Hiebert, 139–40.

[10]White and Blue, *Healing the Wounded*, 40.

[11]*Christianity Today*, March 19, 1990.

[12]*Ministries Today*, January/February 1990.

[13]*National Catholic Reporter*, June 21, 1991.

[14]Ibid.

[15]Ibid.

[16]*Fidelity*, June 1991.